OXFORD IN ONE AFTERNOON

A PRACTICAL GUIDE TO TOUR THE CITY ON FOOT

Renata Lanzoni

Published by Renata Lanzoni

Second Edition in Colour

ISBN: 9798601924740

Copyright © Renata Lanzoni 2020 – All rights reserved

Renata Lanzoni has asserted her right under the Copyright, Designs and Patents Act 1988 to be identified as the author of this work.

All rights reserved. No part of this publication may be reproduced, stored in a retrieval system, or transmitted in any form or by any means, electronic, mechanical, photocopying, recording or otherwise, without the prior permission of the copyright owner.

Content

Introduction 1
Practical Advice 2
When to Visit Oxford 3
The Different Itineraries 4
Points of Interest 5
Main Tour 11
Tour A: Castle 64
Tour B: Christ Church 71
Tour C: Botanical Garden and Punting 83
Tour D: New College 88
Tour E: Natural History and Pitt Rivers Museums ... 93
Tour F: Exeter College 97
The Harry Potter Connection 99
40 Facts about Oxford 104
List of Colleges in 2019 112
Author's Note
Other Books by the Author

Introduction

From an ancient university to Alice in Wonderland, from the Lord of the Rings, to punting in the river, Oscar Wilde to Rowan Atkins, the Mini factory to the dreaming spires, from sharks to tortoises, wild horses to deer, Oxford has so much to offer that it is a must to include in your travel plans.

Touring Oxford in one afternoon is an ambitious task. The amount of history, art, legends and tales to be absorbed is no mean feat, but it can be done. Despite its well-deserved fame and well-known position in the world's culture, Oxford's main sites are concentrated in a relatively small area, very well accessible on foot and possible to be covered in a few intense hours.

In this guide, I will take you on a main tour, which should last approximately two hours and has no costs involved. I will also point you toward the possibility of branching off and then rejoining the main tour on several occasions. For each additional tour option, I will indicate how long it is likely to take so that you can gauge whether to tackle it. I will also let you know if there are any costs involved.

If you did all of the additional tours and the punting trip, your stay in Oxford would stretch to between six and seven hours. But fear not, you can always stop by one of the many watering holes in the city and rest your weary feet for a while before setting off exploring again. The choice of how long to stay in the "City of Dreaming Spires," what to visit and how much to spend is entirely yours. Depending on the time availability, your stamina and the weather, you can spend as little or as long as you choose to discover this fascinating gem of a city.

Welcome to Oxford!

Practical Advice

- Parking in Oxford is an abysmal affair. Try to avoid it at all costs. If you are making your way to Oxford by car, please consider using the Park & Ride facilities that are available just on the outskirts of town. From there, buses will take you into the city centre regularly.

- If you are coming from London, there are frequent trains from both Paddington and Marylebone. The direct trains take around one hour.

- From London, you can also travel to Oxford on a coach. The Oxford Tube (the coach/bus from London) runs very frequently and will drive you all the way to the heart of Oxford in less than two hours, traffic permitting. With pickup points at the main tourist and underground spots in the capital, these coaches are a good alternative to the train.

- Direct buses run to Oxford from all main airports around London, too.

- There are plenty of shops and supermarkets in the area covered by your Oxford tour, so you do not need to stock up on food and drinks beforehand.

- Wear comfortable clothing and shoes as you will be walking for a considerable time.

- Check the weather forecast and prepare accordingly.

When to Visit Oxford

Oxford is famous for its University and Colleges, so it is advisable to take the time to visit inside one of these institutions, to get the feel of what they are about. To do this, it is better if your tour is in the afternoon, as most colleges are not open to visitors in the mornings.

As for which college to visit, the choice is really up to you, the opening times and what your interests are. Many colleges either line the route of the main tour or are easily reachable with a small de-tour. I will highlight which ones you could visit as we go along. Bear in mind that some colleges charge visitors a fee. Opening times also vary depending on the time of the year, and closures due to functions are very common. If your heart is set on a particular college, please check their website to ensure they are open on the day of your tour.

Oxford is busy year round, so it is difficult to suggest a time for a visit, although July and August are the peak tourist months and it is pretty impossible to have a picture taken without anyone else in it. Having said that, they are probably the months when the weather is a bit more clement, although this is not necessarily always so. This is England, after all!

So check your chosen college opening time, the weather forecast and be prepared to have unknown faces in your photographs. You are all set to go.

~ Oxford in One Afternoon ~

The Different Itineraries

In this guide I will highlight one main itinerary with six more that branch off it at different points before rejoining it.

Places of interests are pointed out and discussed as we move along the streets. When the option of branching off to a longer tour presents itself, I will let you know, so you can follow the part of the guide related to that additional tour.

The main tour will take at least a couple of hours. The duration of each additional tour is indicated in the section dedicated to it. If you were to take all of the tours suggested in this guide, your stay in Oxford would stretch to between six and seven hours.

Oxford attracts many fans of Harry Potter because it was used as the setting for the films and inspiration for the books. There is a section in this guide dedicated to the Harry Potter connection in Oxford. In the tours, a reference to this section will be made using the **HP** connotation and number, so you can refer to the appropriate part of the guide.

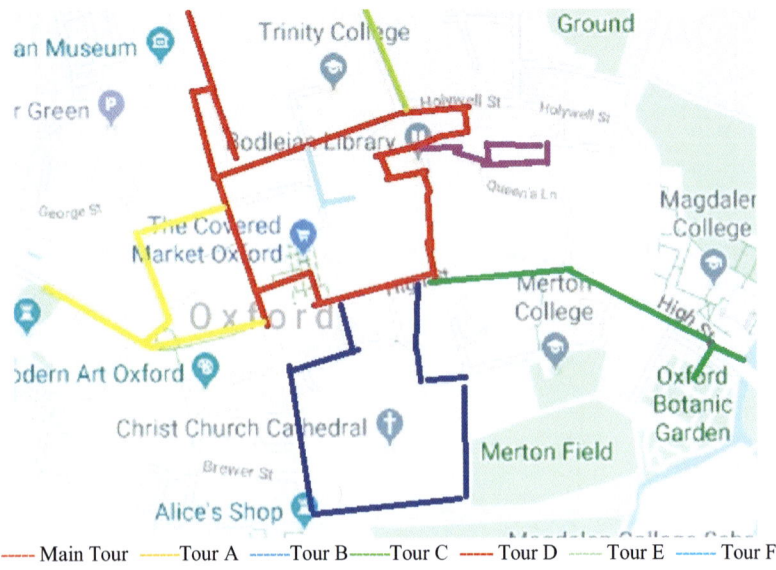

----- Main Tour ——— Tour A ------ Tour B ——— Tour C ---- Tour D ——— Tour E ——— Tour F

Points of Interest

These are the sights covered during the tours:

MAIN TOUR

1. Colleges and University
2. Randolph Hotel
3. Ashmolean Museum
4. Oxford Martyrs Memorial
5. Limestone buildings
6. Cabmen's Shelter
7. Eagle and Child
8. St John's College
9. Saxon Tower
10. Tudor House
11. St Michael of the North Church
12. Ship Street
13. Carfax
14. Swindlestock Tavern

15. Tom Tower
16. Town Hall
17. Covered Market
18. All Souls Church
19. Salutation Tavern and Golden Passage
20. The Mitre
21. C.S. Lewis
22. University Church
23. Radcliffe Square
24. Radcliffe Camera
25. All Souls College
26. Brasenose College
27. Bodleian Library
28. Central Quad of the Bodleian Library
29. Divinity School
30. Bridge of Sighs
31. Sheldonian Theatre
32. Clarendon Building
33. Turf Tavern
34. Bath Place
35. Indian Institute
36. King's Arms
37. Weston Library
38. Front of Clarendon Building and Bearded Heads
39. History of Science Museum
40. Blackwell's
41. White Horse
42. Anthony Gormley Statue
43. Oxfam
44. Execution Cross

A - CASTLE TOUR

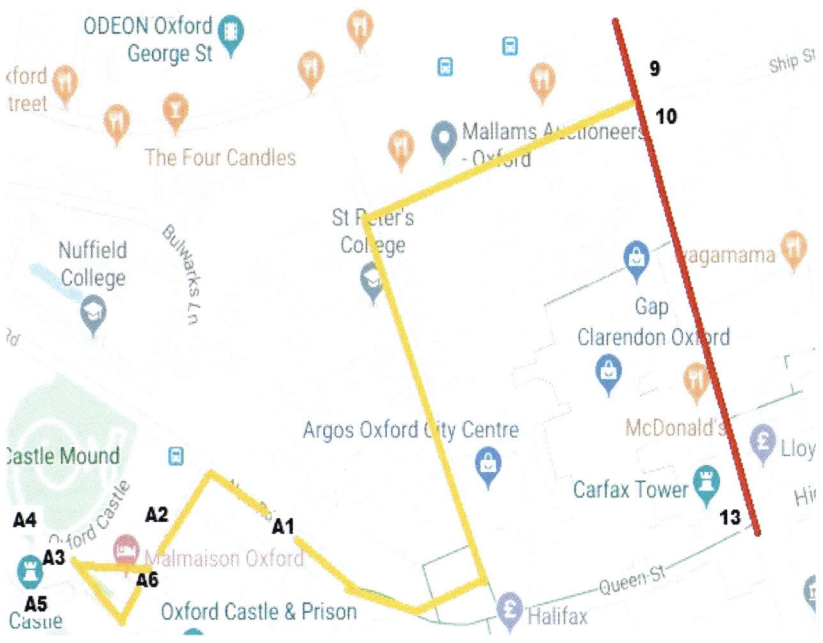

A1. County Hall
A2. Oxford Castle and Prison
A3. George Tower
A4. St Frideswide
A5. Timeline
A6. Malmaison

B - CHRIST CHURCH TOUR

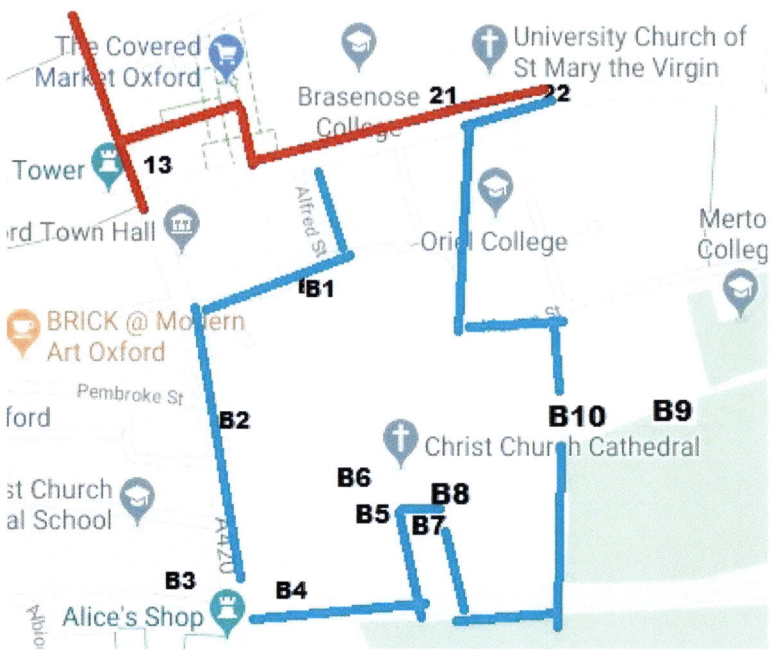

B1. The Bear
B2. Tom Tower
B3. Alice's Shop
B4. Memorial Garden and Christ Church Meadow
B5. Christ Church Stairs
B6. The Dining Hall
B7. No Peel Graffiti
B8. The Cathedral
B9. Dead Man's Walk
B10. Merton Grove Kissing Gate

C - BOTANIC GARDEN AND PUNTING TOUR
C1. Magpie Lane
C2. Queen's Lane Coffee House
C3. Examination Hall
C4. Magdalen Tower and Magdalen College
C5. Botanical Garden
C6. Punting

D - NEW COLLEGE TOUR
D1. Dining Hall
D2. Garden and Walls
D3. Chapel
D4. Cloister

E - NATURAL HISTORY AND PITT RIVERS MUSEUM TOUR
E1. Natural History Museum
E2. Pitt Rivers Museum
E3. Keble College
E4. University Parks

F – EXETER COLLEGE TOUR
F1. Turl Street
F2. Chapel
F3. Fellows' Garden

~ Oxford in One Afternoon ~

HP HARRY POTTER CONNECTION

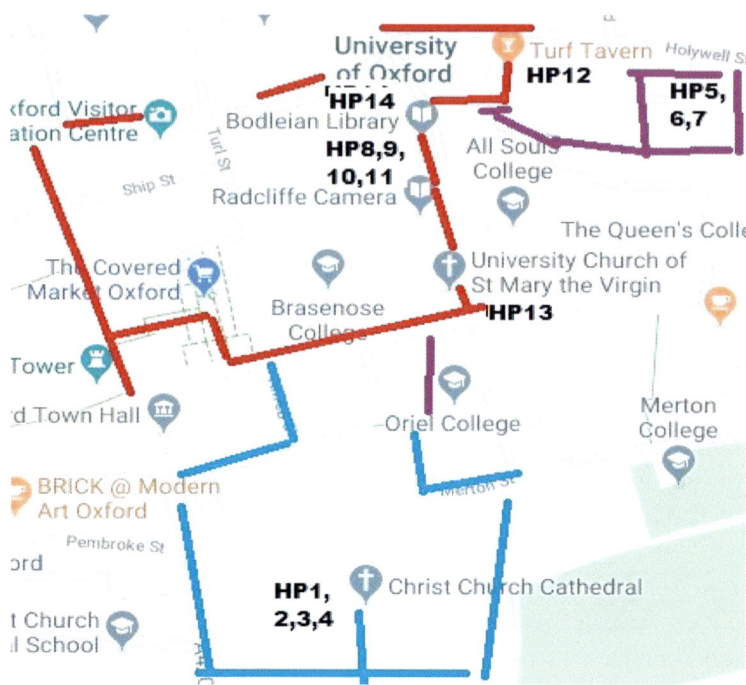

HP1. Great Hall
HP2. Staircase
HP3. Christ Church Cloister
HP4. Baptism Font
HP5. New College Cloister
HP6. New College Corridors
HP7. Old City Walls and Garden
HP8. Divinity School
HP9. Thomas Bodley's Chest
HP10. Duke of Humphrey's Library
HP11. Duke of Pembroke
HP12. Turf Tavern
HP13. University Church
HP14. Sheldonian Theatre yard
HP15. Quidditch
HP 16. Emma Watson

Main Tour

Find your way to Beaumont Street and start your tour just outside the Randolph Hotel, in front of the Ashmolean Museum.

1. Before we move on, it is important to understand the relationship between **colleges and the university** in Oxford,

so here comes a bit of simplified history.

Oxford is the second oldest university in the Western world (the first one is the University of Bologna, in Italy, which was founded in 1088). Records of lessons being held in Oxford date back to 1096, but there were possibly educational institutions in the city before that, too. Until Henry II, however, the English high class was educated in France. Henry II changed all that. He forbade English people to go and study in France and forced education to be provided on English territory. And what better place to develop as an academic centre than a city where education was already established?

But Oxford was not only that, it was also the city where the King himself lived and where both his sons, Richard the Lionheart and the future King John (the one who signed the Magna Carta in 1215) were born. There was in fact a palace, now unfortunately long gone, precisely on the road you are standing now, which was called the King's House, or Beaumont Palace. The palace was built by Henry I, son of William the Conqueror,

and grandad of Henry II. A small stone plaque, together with the name of the street, is all that now remains of the palace.

So Oxford became the main place where lectures were held. The affluent society of England descended on the little thriving commercial town of Oxford in big numbers, and problems arouse immediately. **"Town versus Gown"**, i.e. local people against academics (as the gown is the garment used by university scholars), is a term that has defined the centuries of fights and riots, blood and horrors which followed.

In the beginning, university students and professors were housed in the city and mingled with local people. One accident, though, was pivotal to a radical change that defined the university life in Oxford and more. In 1209, a local lady was killed. As a result, two academics were executed without trial. This caused widespread panic amongst the university population, who felt they needed protection from the local

people. Hence colleges started being built. Students and tutors could eat, pray, study and sleep in the new structures, therefore ensuring their safety. All colleges have, in fact, accommodation rooms, a chapel, a library and dining facility, as well as common rooms.

The relationship between colleges and the university is unique to Oxford and Cambridge. Here colleges and the university co-operate like a federation. To make it easier to understand, consider colleges as the place where students live, while their lessons take place in the university building that houses the faculty of their chosen subject. So lectures are held at the university facilities for the students belonging to the various colleges.

The other unique feature of Oxford and Cambridge universities is the tutorial system they are based on. Not only students attend lessons at the faculties, they also have to attend tutorials, which are very intense lessons held within the colleges by in-house tutors. During tutorials students are either alone or with a maximum of two other students with a professor, and subjects are explored in depth.

Another noteworthy event that ensued from the same fatal killing of 1209, is that a group of professors were so scared that they decided Oxford was no longer safe for them, so they ran away to Cambridge and founded the university there.

Cambridge is therefore about 150 years younger than Oxford, and with 31 colleges, it is smaller than its older counterpart (there are 39 colleges in Oxford).

As for which is the oldest college in Oxford, there are three contenders: Balliol College, Merton College and University College. As all three date back to the mid-1200s, it is hard to say with certainty which is the oldest.

Oxford and Cambridge had a monopoly over English education for centuries, as no other universities were allowed to be founded until the early 1800s. An attempt in 1333 from dissatisfied Oxford students to set up a university in Stamford, Lincolnshire, was repressed by the King, under pressure from Oxford and Cambridge who felt that new universities would encourage dissenting ideas, cause separation within the country and take money away from the ones already established. These were unacceptable possibilities. *Oxbridge* (the term used for the two universities combined) had the backing of royalty to remain the only educational institutions.

2. The **Randolph Hotel** covers a wide area on both Beaumont Street and Magdalen Street. It is one of the oldest standing hotels in modern Oxford. A five-star establishment, it dates back to 1866 and shows a simplified gothic façade. The hotel was named after Dr. Francis Randolph, an eighteenth- century university benefactor. The hotel is featured in several *Inspector Morse* and *Lewis* episodes, and if you just pop inside and turn left, you will find yourself in the "Morse Bar".

3. The **Ashmolean Museum** in front of you is an example of classical style building completed between 1841 and 1845 to house the ever-growing collection of the original Ashmolean Museum. This was first opened in 1683 and located in a building on Broad Street that now hosts the History of Science Museum (see point **39**). The Ashmolean Museum is unique in that it was the first museum owned by the University but purposely built to be open to the public.

4. Keep the Randolph on your right and the Ashmolean on your left and walk to the corner of Magdalen Street and Beaumont Street. In front of you there is the **Memorial to the Oxford Martyrs**.

We need a bit more simplified history here. Henry VIII had six wives (divorced, beheaded, died, divorced, beheaded, survived). Henry had a daughter, Mary, with his first wife, Catherine d'Aragone, but he really wanted a son (and was infatuated with Anne Boleyn), so he sent his right-hand man, Cardinal Wolsey, to ask the Pope's permission to divorce Catherine. Wolsey came back with the Pope's refusal, which made the Cardinal now unpopular with Henry. The King, however, did not take no for an answer and decided to set up his own Church (the Protestant Church), make himself head of it and give himself the right to divorce. Job done!

Henry then married Anne Boleyn and she became pregnant straight away, but gave birth to a daughter, Elizabeth.
Things between Henry and Anne hit difficult times, so much so that Henry had her tried for adultery and decapitated. His third wife, Jane  Seymour, bore him a son, Edward (VI), who unfortunately was not very well. Edward ascended to the throne very young after the death of his father, and continued to promote the Protestant Church. He, however, died only a few years later, and his half-sister Mary I, Henry's first daughter, succeeded him to the throne. Being the daughter of a fervent Catholic and being a devoted Catholic herself, Mary set about to reverse her father's change of church. The quickest way to bring England back to Catholicism was to eliminate all higher officers of the Protestant Church. And so she did. Bishops and archbishops were tried for heresy and burned at the stake. The years 1555 and 1556 saw many executions. Notoriously for Oxford, Bishop Ridley, Bishop Latimer and Archbishop Cranmer were executed on Broad Street. A cross in the middle of the street marks the spot where they were burnt at the stake (see point **44**). All in all,

Mary had about 300 people executed in this way, gaining the notorious nickname *Bloody Mary*.

After Mary, her half-sister, Elizabeth I, came to the throne and set about reversing that process. She wanted the Church of England back. Although she did not have as many people killed as Mary, she too, carried out several executions.

The spire monument you see in front of you is a memorial to the Oxford Martyrs, both Catholics and Protestants, executed in the city of Oxford. We will find a few more memorials in their names as we discover the city.

5. Beyond the Martyrs' Memorial is Balliol College, on its left is a secondary exit of Trinity College, and then St. John's College, three of the most renowned colleges in Oxford. As you can see, the material used to build the colleges is local **limestone**. Most of the older colleges and university buildings were built using this material. The older buildings having been built from materials coming directly from Headington Quarry, now an area included in the city of Oxford itself. Limestone is beautiful, honey-coloured, very iconic, and easy to carve but incredibly unpractical. As it is porous and soft, it absorbs pollution and is easily corroded by the acid rain and all the chemical pollutants in the air; for the same reason, it is also extremely difficult to clean. As we walk along this magical city, you will notice buildings of different shades of "honey-colour" and you will also see the damage and corrosion the stones have suffered.

6. (Please note: if it is before 1 pm, consider adding points **6**, **7** and **8** to the end of your tour, after point **44**, and go now to point **9** instead). If it is past 1pm and you have checked whether St. John's College is open to visitors for the day, cross the road toward Balliol College and turn left, walking along St. Giles. You will see a small wooden  structure currently being used as Najar's Place, a refreshment spot. This shack is, in fact, an historical structure, built in 1895 as a **Cabmen's Shelter**, after the first wooden structure was destroyed. Throughout the years it served many purposes, amongst which it was used as a temporary police station during St. Gile's Fair (a yearly event that takes place the first Monday and Tuesday of September) in the early 1900s.

7.   The pavement widens past Najar's Place. Climb a couple of steps on the left and stand near the gate toward the road. You will see the Taylor Institute side of the Ashmolean Museum in front of you. On the same side of the road, farther right along St. Giles, you will see a light blue oval sign with a red/orange eagle on it. That is the **Eagle and Child** pub, a famous meeting point for the Inklings, the group of writers headed by J.R.R. Tolkien and C.S. Lewis, who used to meet weekly for years in the mid-twentieth century.

8.   Behind you is **St. John's College**, the richest college in Oxford with an alleged fortune of over £630 million pound sterling. It is said that until 1910, you could walk from St. John's College in Oxford to St. John's College in Cambridge without leaving the ground of the college!
If the college is open to visitors, it is usually free to enter. Walk in and you will find yourself in the first quad (or quadrilateral) of the college. Most of the older colleges are built around quads,

either one or more, depending on the ground and wealth available. Students' and tutors' accommodation, library, chapel and dining facilities can all be found around the quad.

Take some time to absorb the atmosphere, walk through the quad and into the next quad ahead of you. The lower part was influenced by Italian classic architecture, as you can see.

The upper floor is adorned by faces and figures. You can see similar Gargoyles and Grotesques (see *40 Facts about Oxford* for definition) almost everywhere in Oxford.

Walk through the second quad and into the garden beyond. Soak in the peace and tranquillity. You could be anywhere; hard to believe you are in the middle of a buzzing city.

It is difficult to understand how green the city of Oxford is as you walk along its street but imagine taking an aerial picture. As the majority of the city centre is occupied by colleges –with their grassy quads and sizable gardens, as well as detached sports grounds -and there is also the huge University Park just in the centre, Oxford is an incredibly green city!

Make your way back to the first quad. Looking at the main entrance, turn right. Through a passage, you can access the chapel via a door on the right. This is a beautiful, peaceful space still very much used. Notice how the seating arrangements face each other rather than the front as in churches. This is normal for college chapels and helps with the acoustics during choir practice.

9. As you leave St. John's College, turn left and continue past the Martyrs' Memorial. Turn right at the junction and then immediately left onto Cornmarket Street. Stop at the corner of St Michael Street, and with your back to the shop, admire the **Saxon Tower**. This is the oldest surviving building in Oxford, dating back to 1040. It stands where the North Gate of the Saxon city used to be. It was a bastion part of the city wall which ran around the original town of Oxford. There was an arch attached to the tower and cells above it: the Bocardo Prison, over the North Gate. Here is where Latimer, Ridley and Cranmer  (point 4) were imprisoned after their heresy trial, and it was from here that Cranmer witnessed the other two being burned alive on Broad Street (point **44**). The Bocardo Prison and North Gate were demolished in 1771 to make traffic flow more easily in the city.

22

NORTH VIEW OF BOCARDO, 1770.

10. Still in front of you, to your right, on the corner of Ship Street, you can find a perfect example of **Tudor architecture**. As you can see, the wooden structure has adjusted and modified since it was built in 1400, but it is still standing and in full use. The lower floor is smaller and the structure expands on the upper floors. This is because taxes were levied on the size of the ground floor.

The shape meant that houses were quite close to each other in the narrow medieval streets. Imagine the whole of Oxford being built like this. And London was the same...until 1666, when the Great Fire of London destroyed nearly 90% of the capital in three days. After that, buildings had to be made only of stone and were not allowed to lean outward.

11. Just beyond and attached to the Saxon Tower is **St. Michael of the North Gate**. A church has been here since around the year 1000 and the Saxon Tower (point **9**) was part of it. The church you see here today dates back to the 1300s and it is now the City Church of Oxford, where the Mayor and Members of the Council of Oxford are expected to worship.

It is from the pulpit of this church that in 1726 John Wesley delivered the famous speech that gave birth to the Methodism, one of today's major Protestant denominations.

This quaint little church is definitely worth a visit. As you get inside and turn right toward the lectern, notice the stained-glass window on your left depicting St. Michael slaying the dragon. This is a memorial for the soldiers who died in the First World War (1914-18). Oxford lost a very high percentage of its academic population during the Great War.

Proceed further into the church and notice the organ. While most of them only have vertical pipes, this has got some horizontal ones, too.

As you cross to the opposite side of the church, you will notice a fourteenth-century **baptismal font**. This used to be in St. Martin Church at Carfax (see point **13**). When that church was demolished in 1896, the font was relocated first to All Souls Church, until it was deconsecrated in 1971, and then here. The font has not only an architectural value but an historical connotation, too. A bit

~ Oxford in One Afternoon ~

further down Cornmarket Street there used to be the Salutation Inn, just past the Golden Cross Passage to the Covered Market (see point **17**). That is where Shakespeare used to stop over on his trips from Stratford to London. The landlord, John Davenant, and his wife, Jane, were good friends of his, so much so that they asked him to be the godfather of their son, also named William. The baptism took place in St. Martin's church, and the font now in St. Michael of the North Gate is the one used by Shakespeare to baptise his godson.

From this church a ceremony called the "beating the bounds" is held each year in May on Ascension Day. This tradition marks out the boundary of the parish. The vicar leads the parishioners around the old boundary stones; and places a cross in chalk on each one. The church wardens then hit the stones with wands made of willow, and shout "mark, mark, mark!" while doing so.

12. Exit St. Michael of the North Church and turn right. Notice the name of the road the church is on. It is **Ship Street**, allegedly an error in copying the real name, *Sheep Street*, so called after the valuable Cotswold wool which was traded here.

HERE YOU CAN BRANCH OFF AND TAKE THE **CASTLE TOUR** (Tour **A**). YOU CAN THEN REJOIN THE MAIN TOUR AT CARFAX TOWER, POINT **13**.

If you are staying on the main tour, take a left onto **Cornmarket Street** and walk along this busy, pedestrian, shopping hub all the way to the crossroads. You will then find yourself in a wide area where four roads meet, with a tower on your right.

13.

The Saxon tower with the clock is at **Carfax.** The name "Carfax" derives from the Latin *quadrifurcus* via the French *carrefour*, both meaning "crossroads". You are in fact standing in the very centre of Oxford. If you look at the map of the city, you will see that it is shaped like a cross, with the tower in its very middle.

This tower used to be attached to St. Martin Church, which was demolished in 1896 to make the road wider. If you look where the clock is, you can see where the roof of the church used to be attached to the tower. Back at point **11**, we mentioned St. Martin already. Here is where Shakespeare baptised his godson. St. Martin was especially important during the centuries of riots and fights between "town and gown", as it was here that "town" people congregated. "Gown" would assemble at University Church, a bit farther along the High Street (see point **22**).

14.

Still standing where you are, notice the building on the corner that houses Santander Bank. This was the site of the **Swindlestock Tavern** (1250-1709). This is where a monumental riot between "town and gown" originated on St

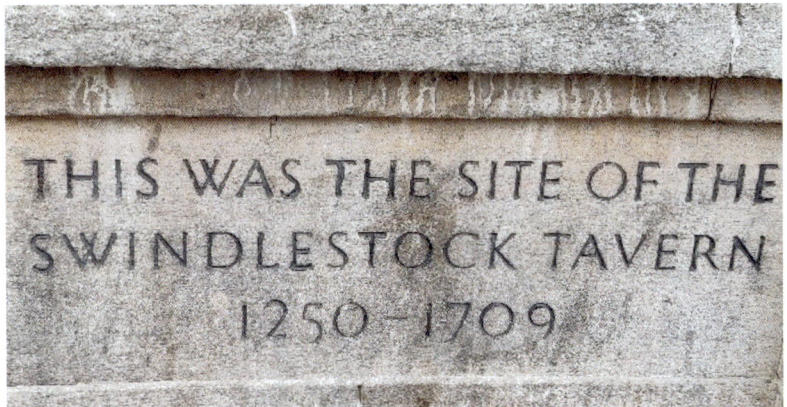

Scholastica Day (10th February) in 1355. What started as a dispute between two students and the landlord, escalated and about 200 students took to the streets. *Town* people poured in from the surrounding areas to take part in the fights. The riot lasted two days, resulted in 63 students dead and possibly 30 *town* people dead too. The situation was eventually resolved in favour of the university and a special charter was created. On St Scholastica Day, the Mayor and Chancellors had to march through the town bare-headed and pay the university a fine of one penny for every scholar killed. This penitence continued for 470 years until in 1825, the Mayor refused to take part.

15. On the pavement, with Carfax Tower behind you, look to your right, down St. Aldates. You will notice an imposing tower on the left-hand side of the road. This is **Tom Tower**, part of Christ Church. It stands at the entrance of the college main quad (Tom Quad). This tower is attributed to Christopher Wren (famous for designing many London landmarks and especially, St. Paul Cathedral). The tower was a late addition to the college, as it was built in the late 1600s, while the college dates back to the early 1500s (more about Christ Church in offshoot tour **B**).

Tom Tower famously rings 101 times at 9:05 p.m. Why these strange numbers? At the time the tower was completed, 101 students studied at the college. As they had to be back in the college at curfew, the bell would ring to ensure they were all back before the doors of the college were closed. But why 9:05 p.m.? Well, you might notice that Oxford is not Greenwich... we are in fact five minutes behind London. So when it is 9:05 p.m.in Greenwich, it is 9 p.m. in Oxford. Yes, I know... However, until the advent of the railway, every city had its own time; it was only when the trains started running, that a common time had to be agreed on.

16.

Still looking in the same direction, but

much closer to where you are standing, you will see the **Town Hall**. This is the third building standing here and covering the same function. A Guildhall built in 1292 was replaced by the

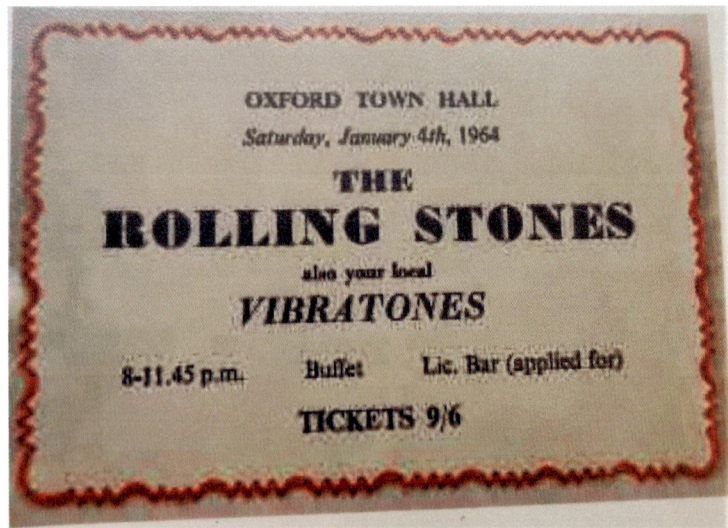

first Town Hall in 1752. In 1891, a design competition was won by local architect Henry Hare with a Jacobean design. The 1752 building was demolished in 1893 and the current building was opened by the then Prince of Wales (later King Edward VII) in May 1897. The new Town Hall building was designed to house not only the central library but the Crown and County Courts as well as the police station. Today, it is the seat of Oxford City Council and a venue for public meetings, entertainment and other events. Famous and less famous bands have played here. It also houses the Museum of Oxford.

The area covered by the Town Hall and all the way to Tom Tower used to be the Jews' settlement until the Jews were expelled from the city in the 1300s.

17. Still standing on the pavement outside Carfax, keep the tower behind you. Ahead of you is the High Street, the main artery to the East. As you look down the High Street, on the left-hand side, you should be able to see some blue

flags with the writing "Covered Market 1774" on them. No price for guessing what is there. However, look behind you. The street now called Queen Street used to be called *Butchers Row*. The road to your right used to be called *Fish (or Fishmongers) Lane* (now St. Aldate's). Now: can you imagine the smell, noise and gore? So in 1774, the University completed its plan for a cleaner and more presentable town. The **Covered Market** was ready and all the stalls that littered the town centre were relocated to the market. Nowadays, you can still find a fishmonger and a couple of butchers in the Covered Market, as well as a store selling fruit and vegetables, but the market is mainly populated by small independent stores and is a real gem. Go and discover it if you have time; it is also especially good if the weather  leaves a lot to be desired, as you can stroll through the four avenues inside, browse the little shops or stop for a bite to eat without being exposed to the elements
.

18. Cross over to stand near Santander bank (to your right) and look along the High Street in front of you. You will see a majestic tower rising to the sky. This used to be **All Souls Church**, which was deconsecrated in 1971 and has been the library of Lincoln College since 1976.

19. Leave Carfax Tower on your left, Lloyds bank on your right, and walk back up Cornmarket Street. On the left hand-side, there is *The Crown Pub*, on the right, there is the Golden Cross Passage. Just on the right of the Golden Passage, still on Cornmarket Street, notice the building. This is number 3 Cornmarket, and it used to be the **Salutation Tavern** (then renamed the Crown Tavern by mid-1600s- do not confuse it with The Crown Pub). This inn used to be run by John Davenant and his wife and is reportedly the place where William Shakespeare used to stop over on his journeys to and from London (see also point **11**).

Enter Golden Passage and you are in a courtyard. This dates back to 1193, when it was called Maugerhall, after the owner, and had shops and an inn on the upper floors. The buildings you see now date back to the late 1400s, when they were used as a coach inn. Where The Crown Pub now stands (on the other side of Cornmarket Street) there used to be the stables.

The Golden Cross courtyard has a strong connection with Shakespeare. This is the site where his plays were occasionally held. Hamlet is known to have been played here.

Keep walking to the end of the courtyard, facing Pizza Express, then take the passage on your left and follow it along. You will end up in the Covered Market. To the left, toward the end of the market there are the fruit and vegetable store, the butchers and the fishmonger; the rest of the market is a mix of eateries and little boutique shops. There are about 60 independent stores huddled in the market, which makes it a good spot to peruse if you are looking for that unusual souvenir.

There are four ways, or *avenues,* in the market that cross it from north to south. Take any one of them and walk toward the exit on the High Street (away from the fruit and veg area).

20.

Now you are on the busy High Street. Turn left, away from Carfax. Pass by the **Mitre Pub** on your left, on the corner with Turl Street.

The Mitre Pub used to be a very busy and active coach inn and has 13th century vaulted cellars. A tunnel used to link the Mitre Inn to the buildings across the High Street. During Henry VIII's Dissolution of the Monasteries, monks were chased into the tunnel and both ends bricked up. Rumour has it that you can still hear their cries if you venture under there.

The present Mitre building dates back to 1630, but there has been an inn on the site since 1300. It has long belonged to Lincoln College, and its name probably derives from the college coat of arms, which depicts the mitre of the Bishop of Lincoln. It was an important coaching inn, and as early as 1671, coaches ran between London and the Mitre on three days a week.

> Passing the Mitre and crossing Turl Street, you will have the old All Souls Church (now Lincoln College's Library -see point **18**) on your left.

21.

Continue down the High Street, past Lincoln College on your left and turn into St. Mary's Passage, stopping just outside the church door on your right. This used to be the main door to St. Mary the Virgin, or University Church. **C.S. Lewis** was a Fellow at Magdalen College and used to come to this church. The story goes that one Sunday morning after service, he exited the church from this door. It had just been snowing but the sky was blue. As he stepped away from the door, he looked to his right and saw the lamppost. He then looked directly in front of him and saw the golden creatures holding up the porch roof, as well as the lion face carved in the door. And lo and behold, when Lucy steps through the wardrobe in the *Chronical of Narnia*, there is snow on the ground, she sees a lamppost and Mr. Tumnus, a strange-looking creature, half-human and half goat. And the rest is history.

Before you move on, take a look at that lamppost. That was actually the first public

36

illumination in the UK and dates back to 1860. Cast iron. Here to outlive us all.

Head back up toward the High Street again and turn left. You will see the main entrance to St. Mary the Virgin Church, also known as University Church.

HERE YOU CAN BRANCH OFF AND TAKE THE **CHRIST CHURCH TOUR** (Tour **B**). YOU CAN THEN REJOIN THE MAIN TOUR AT POINT **22**.

IF YOU WOULD LIKE TO (ALSO) TAKE THE **BOTANICAL GARDEN AND/OR PUNTING TOUR** (Tour **C**), YOU CAN LEAVE THE MAIN ITINERARY NOW AND THEN REJOIN IT AT POINT **22**.

22. This entrance to the **University Church of Saint Mary the Virgin** is a later addition to the building which, in its oldest parts, dates back to the 1200s.

This entrance was added in 1637 by Nicholas Stone, master mason to Charles I. This south porch is very ornate, with spiral columns and a shell niche with a statue of the Virgin and Child.

As well as a chapel in every college, the University provided a main church for all its scholars.

Here is where the academic world congregated and assembled against the "town" if need be. Between here and the now-demolished St. Martin's Church at Carfax (point **13**) many riots took place and much blood was spilled, both from locals and academics.

University Church was at the heart of the walled medieval town, and it is where the University originated from. It is here that the first lectures were given and here that graduation and matriculation ceremonies were held until the Sheldonian Theatre was eventually built in the late 1600s (see point **31**). University Church is also the place where the trials for heresy took place under Mary I and where Latimer, Ridley and Cranmer were condemned to the stake (point **4**).

Here is also where the university library first started, in a back room with nine books.

The oldest part of the church is the tower, which dates back to 1270, while the spire was built in 1320. As you walk through the south door, notice the stained glass windows at the back and on the sides. Walk through the centre and on the other side you will see a black plaque on the wall. This is another memorial dedicated to the Oxford Martyrs, both Protestant and Catholics, who were executed over the years for their religious beliefs (see also point **4** and **44**). Just behind you there is a column with a description of what happened to the Oxford Martyrs and a candle stand. This is "Cranmer Pillar", as during his trial here, a wooden stage was erected for him to stand on and be judged. You can still see the carving on the column made on purpose to support the stage.

Before leaving, step along the chancel, the further part of the church. This has choir stalls that date back to the 15th century

and an impressive, centre-stage, 16th century painting by Francesco Bassano the Younger, an Italian renaissance artist.

HP13.

23. Walk out of the church using the door to the opposite side of where you entered, passing the entrance to the tower. You are now out in the magnificent **Radcliffe Square**. This is one of the most photographed and filmed locations in England. Many period dramas and contemporary movies have been filmed here. This is not only because the place is quite simply stunning, but look around you and you will not be able to spot any modern building. If you removed the bikes and a few dustbins, you could be in the 1700s. The reason for this stands just behind you, in the University Church Spire.

~ Oxford in One Afternoon ~

There is a city planning rule in Oxford that states that no building can be higher than the top of the church spire for a radius of 10 square miles. This means not only that from where you are standing no high buildings can be seen but also that if you felt like a bit of a hike and you climbed to the panoramic terrace of the church tower, the view that opens up to you is amazing.

24.

The round building at the centre of the square is the **Radcliffe Camera** (Camera means *room* in Latin), a building now part of the Bodleian Library and belonging to Oxford University. This building was designed by James Gibbs in neo-classical style and built between 1737 and 1749 to house the Radcliffe Science Library. The construction of the library was funded by a legacy of £40,000 left by John Radcliffe, a fellow of Lincoln College who became a royal physician to William III and Mary II.

In 1861, the Radcliffe Library became part of the Bodleian Library and changed its name to the Radcliffe Camera. The Science Library moved into another building, and the Camera became home to additional reading areas of the Bodleian Library.

In 1863, a new entrance was opened on the north side. Between 1909 and 1912, a two-storey underground book storage area was constructed beneath the north lawn of the library with a tunnel connecting it with the Bodleian Library. This was refurbished in 2011 and is now known as the "Gladstone Link".

25. Enclosing the square from the right is **All Souls College**, the only college in Oxford with no students.

Neither undergraduates nor graduates are admitted here, only fellows. To be accepted as a Fellow of All Souls College, there is a very difficult examination to be passed. The college is very elitist and it is incredibly prestigious to be part of it. Sir Christopher Wren and Lawrence of Arabia are two of the famous fellows of the college. This college is a memorial institution, taking its name from "all the souls" who perished during the 14th century 100-year war with France.

The Sundial on the left-hand side of the quad is attributed to Christopher Wren. The double towers are attributed to Nicholas Hawksmoor, Wren's disciple, who is said to have designed the towers so that they spell W in honour of Wren.

26. To the left of the square, near University Church, there is Lincoln College. A little farther up is **Brasenose College**, and the Fellows' Garden terrace of Exeter College is just north of Brasenose Lane. Brasenose is one of the most curious names in Oxford. The story behind it, is that it stems from a knocker that hung on the door of the original medieval hall that stood on the site the College occupies today. That knocker was made of bronze (brase) and was shaped like a nose (!). During unrests in 1333 a group of students left Oxford and settled in Stamford, in Lincolnshire, bringing the knocker with them. Although the students later returned to Oxford, the knocker did not. In 1890, the college purchased a house put up for sale in Lincolnshire as it held a very familiar knocker. That very same knocker now safely hangs in the dining hall.

27.

Closing off Radcliffe Square to the north is the **Bodleian Library**. From where you are standing, just outside University Church, turn right and then left along Catte Street. All Souls College is on your right. Stop at its gate to admire the beautiful quad and the sundial up on the north wall. Continue along Catte Street, leaving All Souls College on your right. Pass the traffic restriction bar. The road is a bit wider now. On the right, you will find Hereford College and on your left is the magnificent Bodleian Library. Go through its ancient oak doors. These are the original doors and have been here since the 1600s. The colleges in existence in Oxford at the time are represented on these doors by their crests. There is a ticket office on your right as you go through the doors. The library is not open to tourists, but you can purchase their own "in-house" tour here. These tours are very popular, so you might have to buy it for a future date. Alternatively, you can buy a ticket to visit the Divinity School.

This you can do on your own, and I highly recommend it (see point **29**).

28. As you walk into the **Centre Quad** of the library, you will be overwhelmed by the amount of detail to take in. You are now standing at the very heart of the University Library. The university library actually started in the 1200s, in a small back room of the University Church. When the collection got bigger, the Duke of Humphrey built a library above the then-existing Divinity School. Books were destroyed in the years of the Reformation, but when things calmed down, Thomas Bodley, who used to work for Queen Elizabeth, decided to dedicate his retirement to the construction of the University Library. The oldest part was finished in 1610, while the later addition was completed in 1624. Because of what happened with the books during the Reformation, Thomas Bodley was adamant that education should be preserved and books defended. To ensure that culture would be passed down to future generations, he made an agreement with the Royal Stationers, whereby the University Library was to receive a copy of every single book published in the UK. That agreement still stands more than 400 years later, so, as you can imagine, the Bodleian Library now houses more than 12 million books and its collection is growing daily. Because of the high number, the books are stored in several off-site locations, too.

As you stand in the centre Quad and look up at the many Gargoyles and Grotesques adorning the upper floor, you will also see a few TB initials, obviously standing for Thomas Bodley.

On the ground floor, you will notice doors with Latin inscriptions. These were the **original lecture rooms** of the university. Many famous personalities studied and taught in these rooms. Sir Christopher Wren held lessons in the *Schola Astronomiae et Rhetoricae*, in the corner.

Looking back to where you entered the quad, you will notice the beautiful tower. This is called the **Tower of the Five Orders,** and you can see how the columns on the side become more and more complicated as you ascend, from Tuscan to Doric, Ionic, Corinthian and Complex styles.

The big man depicted in the centre is King James I (King James VI of Scotland), who took over the reign of England after Elizabeth I passed away and unified it with Scotland. He is holding two books in his hands: one is the Bible (the translated

English-approved version of the Bible for the Church of England), the other is *Daemonology,* a book he wrote and published in 1597. This book was about demons, witches, werewolves, vampires, etc. The book endorses the practice of witch hunting and in those days, if you had ginger hair, you were left-handed, had a birth mark or a few other oddities, you were believed to be a witch. To prove you were not, you would be thrown in the river with your hands and feet bound. If you drowned, you weren't a witch, but if you survived, you were indeed a witch and would be burned at the stake. The good old days, eh?

Still looking toward the tower, on your left you will see an exit, and over that exit, you can see the University Crest showing the original motto of the university "*Dominus Illuminatio Mea*" (God is my illumination). These days, the University has lost the strict religious connotation, and its motto is now "*Illumination through Education.*"

Opposite the Tower there is the bronze statue of the **Duke of Pembroke**, a literal benefactor who sponsored much of William Shakespeare's work. Behind him is the entrance to the Divinity School. If you purchased your tickets to visit this, please make your way through the glass door and the double wooden doors just in front of you and prepared to be amazed.
HP11

29.
You are now in the **Divinity School**. This is the oldest standing University lecture room, completed between 1427 and 1483. This room was used for theology lessons and was still in use as an examination hall until the late 1900s. These days, it is used for functions, both private and university-related, it is used during matriculation and graduation ceremonies, and also as the setting for many films.

The ceiling took seven years to be carved and you will notice that there are many initials carved into it, as well as the word "God" and "Deus." The bigger the initial, the more money the individual or family gave to the school. It also contains more than 400 bosses (or protrusions) in its vaultings. The door on the right-hand wall was a late addition by Sir Christopher Wren, in the late 1600s. This opening was added to make it easier to join the Divinity School to the (then) new building outside, the Sheldonian Theatre, designed by Sir Christopher Wren (see point **31**). The wooden door opposite the one you entered leads to **Convocation House**, an early 1600s addition that used to house tribunal chambers for the university. Convocation House also served as home for the Royalist Members of the English Parliament during the reign of Charles II.
HP8

Half-way down the left-hand side you will see **Thomas Bodley's Chest**. At the time there were no banks, so Sir Thomas Bodley used to keep his money and important documents in this chest, which travelled everywhere with him. He called this "my blacke iron chest" and left it to the library in his will. The mechanism for locking the chest is very ingenious, as you can see, and the three keys needed to open the chest where entrusted to three different individuals.

HP9

On the opposite side, you will find a wooden chair. This was built in 1662 with wood savaged from the *Golden Hind*, Francis Drake's ship, which had been moored in London since Drake's knighthood in 1581.

Notice on top of the main door you entered from the space of a missing statue, and the statue with the missing head. These were the disfigurations carried out during the reformation. The statue of Jesus was removed and St. Peter's statue was decapitated.

Above the Divinity School is the **Duke of Humphrey's Library**, which you can only visit with the library's tours. This library was the University Library until the Bodleian was built. Constructed around 1480, it held the collection of 280 manuscripts donated by the Duke of Humphrey, the brother of King Henry V. It was a very generous donation at the time, as the university only had 20 books. Today, only three books of the original collection remain, as the Reformation movement in the mid-1500s destroyed most of the books held by the University.

HP10

Upon exiting the Divinity School, take the exit on the left of the quad, under the University Crest.

30. You are now in the centre of a very interesting and busy University space. To your right is a (probably) familiar-looking bridge.

This bridge dates back to 1914, and the story is that a group of professors from Oxford visited Venice and liked the bridge so much, they wanted a copy of it in Oxford. And so it was that Oxford had his first bridge "not on water," and it became known as the **Bridge of Sighs**. Academics from Cambridge saw the

bridge in Oxford and also wanted a copy, so now Cambridge has a copy of a copy of a bridge in Venice. Unfortunately, they all got a bit confused, and the copy is of the Rialto Bridge, not the Bridge of Sighs.
Also, there is a good reason in Venice for the bridge to have such a name. That bridge joins the tribunal to the prison, so convicts passing through it would either be worried about the imminent trial or take the last look at the outside world on their way either to jail or the execution site. There is no such deep meaning in Oxford. The bridge simply joins two buildings belonging to Hertford College.

31. With the Bodleian Library behind you and the Bridge of Sighs on your right, the building on your left is the **Sheldonian Theatre**. This building was commissioned by Gilbert Sheldon, the Chancellor of the University, to Sir Christopher Wren as a building especially dedicated to ceremonies. The name "theatre" is misleading as it was never expected to host shows. The building is modelled on the Roman Theatre of Marcellus. It is horseshoe-shaped and surmounted by a spectacular cupola from which you can see amazing views of the Oxford Spires.

The Sheldonian Theatre was built to host ceremonies, especially matriculation (when students first start life at Oxford) and graduation (when they get their degrees). Both ceremonies are still held here frequently. As you can imagine, with an Oxford University student population of around 24,000, these ceremonies tend to take place quite often. Both matriculation and graduation ceremonies are held in Latin, and students are expected to wear the academic gown and carry the flat hat that they can only wear once the graduation ceremony is over.

The theatre is also at times used for lectures, conferences and musical performances.

To the side toward the Broad Street, the Theatre is guarded by 13 anonymous, bearded figures, sometimes (wrongly) called the Emperors. These are not the originals ones, as those eroded, but date back to 1972. Legend has it that on Christmas day, they come down from their plinths and go for a pint at the White Horse Pub across the road. I have never witnessed it, but that doesn't mean it's not true...
HP14.

32. Still in the open space with the Bodleian behind you, in front of you is the back of the **Clarendon Building**. This was built between 1711 and 1715 by Nicholas Hawksmoor (C. Wren's pupil) to house **Oxford University Press**. Until then, the Press operated from premises under the Sheldonian Theatre, but could not make use of the presses when ceremonies were taking place. The Clarendon Building was constructed to remedy this. However, Oxford University Press soon outgrew its premises and by 1830 a new place was built for them on Walton Street, a few minutes away. The university used the building for administrative purposes until 1975, when the Clarendon Building was transferred to the Bodleian Library.

The big project Oxford University Press took up in their new premises in Walton Street was to compile the **Oxford Dictionary**, the first authority on the English language. This project started in 1857 with the letter "*a*" and four years later, they arrived at the word "*ant*." The whole dictionary was completed and published in 1884, 27 years after the project started.

HERE YOU CAN BRANCH OFF AND TAKE THE **NEW COLLEGE TOUR** (Tour **D**). YOU CAN THEN REJOIN THE MAIN TOUR AT THE TURF TAVERN (POINT **33**)

33.

Now turn right and exit the library area going toward the Bridge of Sighs. Just past the bridge, on the left hand side, you will see Helen's Passage, a small alleyway with the inscription in the picture.

This is the way to the **Turf Tavern**, and its motto is *An Education in Intoxication.* Helen's Passage used to be called Hell's Passage and it was a way out of the town walls. Outside the town walls, police had no jurisdiction and the city laws did not rule. The pub we are going to visit used to be called the Spotted Cow and was a very seedy and infamous place. The new name dates back to 1842 and comes from *Turfmen* or *Turf Accountants* (bookies).

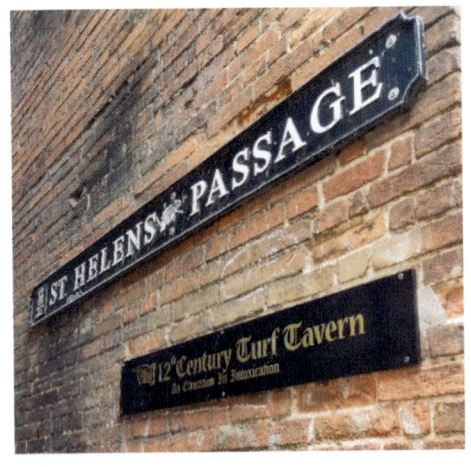

A certain Bill Clinton famously *"did not inhale"* that joint here. And the Australian Prime Minister Bob Hawke set a Guinness Book of World Records for drinking a yard of ale in 11 seconds. For those of us who do not know how much a yard of beer is, it is the equivalent of three pints or 1.4 litres. That record still stands.

Many famous people have stopped at the Turf Tavern throughout the centuries, and the place is featured in many films and has inspired many more. As you get to the pub through the little alleyway, the wall on your right is the original Saxon city wall, more than 1,000 years old, which protected the ancient City of Oxford. It is the very wall that ran all the way to the North Gate, to the tower we first encountered in point **9**.

Leave the wall behind you and turn toward the entrance of the pub. Before leaving it on your right, put your head through the door and feel the age of this place. This pub dates back to the late 1300s.

Now leave the pub on your right, pass its beer garden

and continue through a small covered alleyway that ends up next to a little 17th courtyard.
HP12.

34.

You are now in **Bath Place**. This is a tiny courtyard surrounded by seventeenth-century cottages. These were built in the early sixteen hundreds to house Flemish weavers who were granted permission to build against the outside of the city wall. The name of the place comes possibly from a communal well and bathhouse which are thought to have been located here. Until the 19th century, Bath Place cottages were home to poor people, including Jane Burden, who became a worldwide famous muse. She was born in one of the cottages here, but was spotted by Dante Gabrielle Rossetti, who employed her as a model. She then became the embodiment of female beauty of the Pre-Raphaelite movement, and went on to marry William Morris. Their wedding took place at St. Michael of the North Gate (see point **11**) in 1859.

Bath Place has many more claims to fame. Not only it is mentioned in Thomas Hardy's novel *Jude the Obscure* and was home to the well-known mystery writer and translator of Dante,

Dorothy L. Sayers, but the Hotel also boasts Richard Burton and Elizabeth Taylor amongst the most famous of its guests.

Walk to the road and turn left.

35. Stop at the roundabout at the end of the road. On your left is a building that used to be the **Indian Institute.** You can still see the elephant head on the wall. On the other side of the road is a pub belonging to Wadham College, the Kings Arms.

36. The claim to fame of the **Kings Arms** is that it has the highest IQ per square inch in Oxford, as a lot of students and professors like to drink here. My take on this is that they might very well be right in their claim when the academics walk in, but I very much doubt their fame stands the same when they walk out of the pub a few hours later.

57

HERE YOU CAN BRANCH OFF AND TAKE THE **NATURAL HISTORY AND PITT RIVERS MUSEUM TOUR** (Tour **E**). YOU CAN THEN REJOIN THE MAIN TOUR AT THE WESTON LIBRARY (POINT **37**)

37.

Cross over to the other side of the roundabout, opposite the Kings Arms, and stop in front of the **Weston Library**. This is part of the Bodleian Library and was originally called *New Library* when it was opened in 1946. As the library grew exponentially, new buildings were added. When the New Library was re-opened in 2015, after lengthy refurbishment, it was given the new name of Weston Library after the Weston family who sponsored the major refurbishment.

38. Opposite the Weston Library, on the other side of the road, you can see the front of the Clarendon Building (point **32**), with its giant Doric Portico, and the front of the Sheldonian Theatre, with its bearded heads (point **31**).

39. Next to the Sheldonian Theatre is the **History of Science Museum**. This building was the original site for the Ashmolean Museum and is, at times, attributed to Sir Christopher Wren. The museum was designed to be the first University Museum open to the public and housed the collection of Elias Ashmole. As the museum collection grew, a new building was erected where the Ashmolean Museum is now, on the corner between Beaumont Road and St Giles, where we first started (see point **3**).

40. Continuing along Broad Street, opposite the History of Science Museum, you will see **Blackwell's Bookshop**, allegedly the largest academic and specialist bookshop in England with a collection of more than 150,000 books. This was the very first shop opened by the family business in 1879, and it was originally only twelve square feet. The business grew exponentially though and the shop soon incorporated the upstairs, cellar and neighbouring shops. The Norrington Room was opened in 1966, named after Sir Arthur Norrington, the then-President of the adjoining Trinity College. The Norrington Room extends under the grounds of Trinity College and boasts more than three miles (5 km) of shelving. At 10,000 square feet (930 square metres), this room retains the Guinness Book of Record entry as the largest single room selling books.

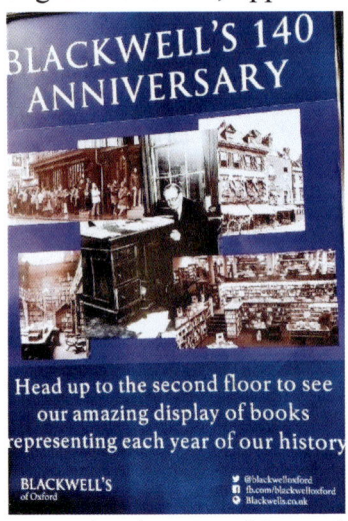

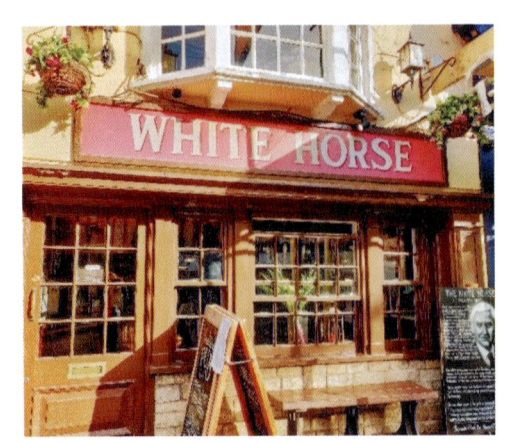

41. As you leave Blackwell's on your right and continue along the pavement, you will pass the **White Horse Pub**, which features in many *Inspector Morse* episodes and which, according to the legend, serves the famous Christmas pint to the bearded heads guarding the Sheldonian Theatre (point **31**). Continuing along, you will pass by Trinity College, with its beautiful grounds. After Trinity, there is Balliol College, one of the three colleges battling for the position of the oldest college in Oxford, together with Merton College and University College (point **1**).

42.

Stop in your step and look across the road, above the new Blackwell's shop. On the roof of Exeter College, you will see a statue of a 7-foot tall naked man. This sculpture, by Anthony Gormley, was given by an anonymous donor to Exeter College and is allegedly inspired by the features of its author.

This statue was erected in 2009. Many more statues by Mr. Gormley have popped up all over London and on the beaches of England, and many have caused quite a reaction from the public as they seem so real. One of them, for example, is near a bridge and police have received many calls from people concerned that someone was about to jump in the river. Likewise, one of the statues is on a roof ledge and collects water. On one occasion, a lady called the police complaining someone urinated on her.

HERE YOU CAN BRANCH OFF AND TAKE THE **EXETER COLLEGE TOUR** (Tour **F**). YOU CAN THEN REJOIN THE MAIN TOUR AT THE OXFAM SHOP (POINT **43**).

43. Continue on passing the beautiful grounds of Trinity College on your right. Across the road, you will notice the **Oxfam Shop**. Oxfam stands for *Oxford against Famine,* and it was formed in 1942 after a meeting held at University Church. The shop you see here is the first shop of the charity chain, and it dates back to 1947. Now, Oxfam has approximately 650 shops worldwide.

44. Proceeding along the same pavement, notice the **cross in the middle of the road**. This marks the spot where Bishop Ridley, Bishop Latimer and Archbishop Cranmer were burned at the stake by Mary I (see point **4**).
There is a **plaque** commemorating them on the wall of Balliol College. As you can see, Latimer and Ridley were executed in 1555. Cranmer watched them being burned, from his cell in the Bocardo Prison, at the North Gate (see point **9**). Because of that and the tortures he endured, he recanted his faith and therefore was not executed till 1556, when he declared himself guilty of

still being a Protestant. He allegedly put his right hand in the flames first and watched it burn, as it was with his right hand that he signed the recantation letter renouncing his faith.

Wooden doors to the college used to stand where the plaque now is. These were very badly damaged by the intensity of the fires and were removed and used internally.

Pass the plaque on your right and continue toward Debenhams.

Round the first corner into Magdalen Road East, and in a few steps you will find yourself back at the Oxford Martyrs' Memorial you started from (point **4)**. Many tourists are told that the Memorial is the spire of a sunken church and that if you descend the stairs you see on your left, you will find yourself in the church. If you descend those stairs, you will find yourself in the public toilets…

Please note, if you started the tour before 1 p.m., you had to bypass points **6**, **7** and **8** at the beginning. You could now follow those steps of the tour, by just continuing along the road.

I hope you enjoyed your tour!

Tour A: Castle

Add an extra 20 minutes to the main tour. No cost.

*From point **12** of the main tour*, cross Cornmarket Street and dive into St Michael Street.

Walk past the Oxford Union on your left, where eminent personalities often make speeches, and head to the end of the street.

At the end, turn left into New Inn Hall Street and follow it to the end, until you come out into Bonn Square, facing the Westgate Shopping Centre. Turn right, cross the road at the pedestrian crossing just outside the 1960s County Council building and continue right onto New Road.

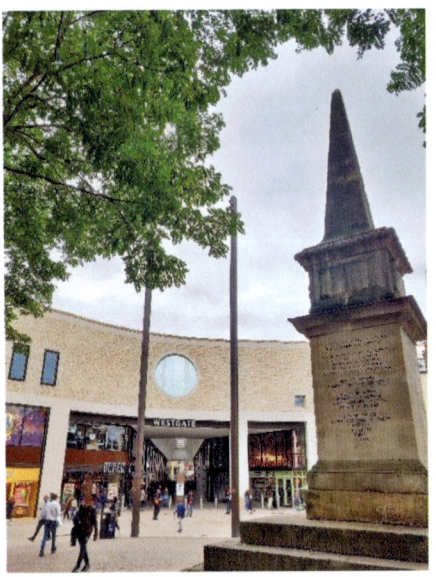

A1. On your left, there is the 19th century **County Hall**, a Gothic Revival style building, originally built as a facility to dispense justice. It was then used to house County Council meetings. There is a tunnel that joins the County Hall to the building behind it. That building used to be the prison and the castle.

A2. Walk just a few yards farther on and you will find an opening on your left. You can see the *Malmaison Hotel* right in front of you. Enter the courtyard. This is the site of the **Oxford Castle and Prison**. This was a functional, working prison until 1996 when it was closed and renovated for ten years. Before it was opened to the public in 2006, law-abiding citizens of Oxford had never seen behind the perimeter wall.

~ Oxford in One Afternoon ~

Pass the *Slug & Lettuce* bar on your right, and turn right through the opening, then left. In front of you there is a mound. This was the original castle structure. A motte and bailey fortification with a wooden building at the top, of which unfortunately nothing remains. Walk along the mound and head for the Visitor Centre entrance at the far end.

A3. Above, in front of you, **St. George's tower** dominates

the complex. Thought to have been part of the old city wall and the site of the West Gate of the old Saxon town, it was then incorporated into the castle complex. Just outside the entrance to the Visitors' Centre, you will see a timeline on the ground starting from the year 700. This tells the events that shaped Oxford in general and the castle in particular. Walk along it and you will learn a few interesting facts.

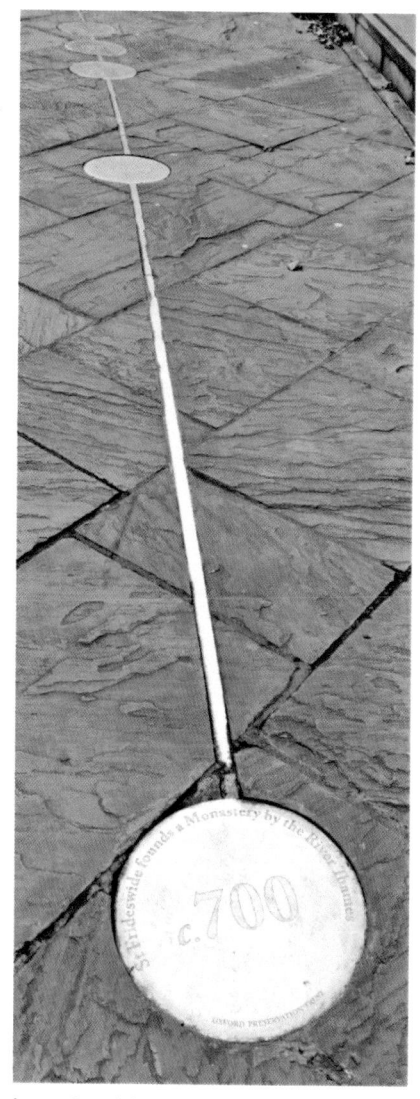

A4. As you can see, it appears that Oxford was founded by **St. Frideswide**. The very simple version of the legend goes that Frideswide was the daughter of a local king. Once her father died, she was pursued by a rather unpleasant king. She desperately wanted to become a nun and was not in the least interested in the king. She ran away toward where Oxford now stands and he went in hot pursuit. However, when he approached Oxford, he lost his sight. Frideswide told him she could restore his vision if he promised to leave her alone. He promised, got his sight back and left her. She then founded a Priory. From then on, the monastery grew and with it the need for educational establishments. Hence, Oxford established itself as a centre of knowledge. The site of Frideswide's old monastery is where Christ Church (see tour **B**) now stands. On building the college, the old priory was destroyed, but parts of the old church remain and have been incorporated into the college chapel (which is also the Cathedral of Oxford). It is debatable, however, whether a settlement already existed on the site of present day Oxford before St Frideswide founded her Priory. If nothing existed prior to Frideswide's monastery, maybe the city would now be called something on the line of Frideswideford. As it isn't, it is likely that a town already existed by the time she came and settled here.

As you continue along the timeline on the floor of the castle yard, you will see that the castle underwent several modifications, extensions and expansions throughout the centuries, and that it was designated as a county jail as early as 1239.

Over the centuries the upkeep of the castle and the prison was given in charge to local families who generally did not have the knowledge nor the inclination to look after it. Continuous disrepair meant prisoners were able to escape on several occasions.

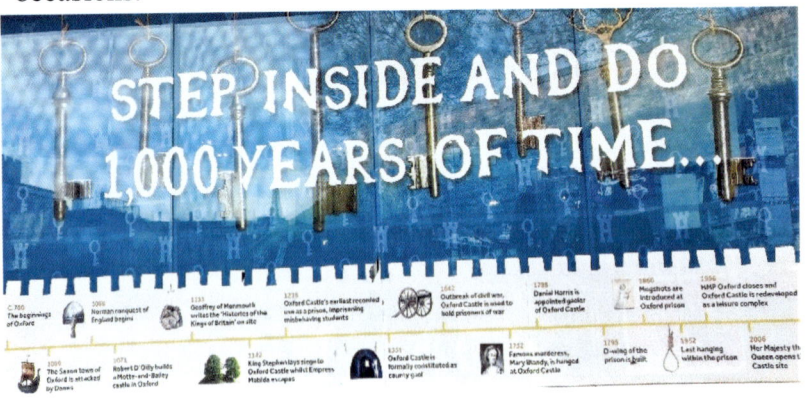

A5. As you move along the **timeline**, you will come to 1643, and the mention of the Civil War. This begs a little history paragraph. When Charles I ran away from London with his men and Oliver Cromwell in hot pursuit, he came to Oxford. The University town was Royalist and stood behind the King. King Charles established himself at Christ Church and held his Parliament sessions in the dining hall of the college (see tour **B**).

Between 1642 and 1646, Oxford was designated the capital of England by the King.

Oliver Cromwell was stationed just outside the city, waiting for his chance to seize the King. He had to wait a few years, but the "town" people supported him.

Moving along the timeline, you will come to 1863, when the last public execution was held where you are standing. After that, the castle was just used as the county prison, until its renovation and transformation between 1996 and 2006, which has resulted in what it is today: a space for all to enjoy.

A6. When you get to the end of the timeline, you will be near the side entrance to the **Malmaison hotel**, ahead and to your right. Go in there, through the glass door and turn right. Pass reception and up a few steps and you find yourself in the prison. If you are lucky enough to find some of the rooms being cleaned, ask the staff if you can take a quick look inside.

What was then a dreary place is now a very posh hotel. Guests pay for the privilege of spending the night in prison cells. The rooms are the result of a merger of three original cells to give you a luxury bedroom and a super bathroom. The doors are still the original ones, though.

With the steps from reception behind you, turn right and descend the flight of stairs. Out of the two sets of doors at the bottom of the stairs, turn right and in the corner, you will be presented with an original prison cell. Well worth visiting to get the feeling of what must have been like to be a guest of HM Queen.

Follow the dark corridor to the end and through a wooden door you are now in the restaurant. Take a look around and check out how this now-modern space was carved out of the original prison structure. When you are ready, take the steps up and go out of the glass emergency door. You are now in the castle courtyard. Go through the archway in front of you, and you are back on the front of the hotel.

Leave the castle from where you entered. Back past the County Hall, cross the road and walk past the Westgate Shopping Centre, leaving it on your right. Continue along Queen Street, pass Marks and Spenser, and stop on the pavement at the crossroad with Cornmarket Street.

Now please rejoin the main tour at point **13**.

Tour B: Christ Church

Add an extra 30 minutes to the main tour if only visiting the Meadow or at least an additional hour if visiting the college as well – it is advisable to book tickets for the college online to avoid lengthy queues, especially in the summer months..

There is a cost for visiting the college. At the time of writing this guide, the price is £15 per person.

B1. From point **21** of the main tour.

Cross over High Street at the pedestrian traffic light and dive into Alfred Street. At the end, on the corner, peep into **The Bear Inn**. This is one of the oldest pubs in Oxford. You will notice a considerable collection of ties. The tradition is that you can have a drink in exchange for a piece of your tie.

Turn right at the end of Alfred Street onto Blue Boar Street and walk to the end of the road. You will end up on St. Aldates; turn left without crossing the road and walk down this main artery. On your right, you will see the main post office and then St. Aldates church.

~ Oxford in One Afternoon ~

B2. On your left and above you is Tom Tower (see point **15**

of the main tour). Through the gate under the tower, you can see **Tom Quad** of Christ Church – the biggest quad in Oxford – guarded by the Wardens. This is not the main visitors' entrance to the college. Take some pictures from this view point, though, before moving on.

B3. Continuing down St. Aldates, you'll come to some garden gates on your left. Before diving into them, take a minute to look across the road. You will see the red sign of Alice's Shop. This is related to **Alice in Wonderland**, by Lewis Carroll. Alice was indeed a real girl; her full name was Alice Liddle, daughter of Henry

Liddle, Dean of Christ Church. Lewis Carroll was a professor of mathematics and logic at the college; however, his real name was Charles Dodgson. He was very friendly with the Dean's family and used to spend a lot of his free time with them. On one such occasion, they were having a picnic on the river bank in Christ Church Meadow after a boat outing. Alice wanted a story and in that moment a white rabbit ran into a hole near a tree on the bank. That was the inspiration that led to the world-famous book. The book only got written upon Alice's insistence as Dodgson, being a professor of mathematics, did not want to put his name to a child's book. He, therefore, decided to write it under a pseudonym.

Queen Victoria was a fan of the book and asked Dodgson to send her a copy of his next book. He obliged. However, as his next book was a treatise on mathematical principles; the Queen was none too impressed.

B4. Now, turn into the **Memorial Gardens** on your left. These beautiful gardens were opened in 1926 in memory of all those who lost their lives in the First World War.

You are now in the grounds of Christ Church. Continue along and pass over a small bridge. This is a bridge over a covered stream that used to be the sewage system from the St. Ebbs quarter of the old town. When this stream was being cleaned as part of the works for the Memorial Gardens, the workmen found an unusual "surprise": The remains of a wooden boat with two skeletons dressed in Christ Church Victorian students' clothes were discovered up-stream. Curiosity really does not pay sometimes.

Pass the stream and you will find yourself in **Christ Church Meadow**, with the college on your left.

If you are lucky, you will see some English long-horned cattle in the meadows. These belong to the college. The grounds run all the way to the river, and if you have time and energy, it is worth the walk.

B5. If you decide to visit the college, buy your ticket from the Visitors' Centre on your left and make your way to the entrance. Your tour is pre-organised; you just need to follow the directions marked for visitors, once you get inside the college. When you walk in, take a look at the gothic gargoyles and grotesques adorning the courtyard. They are quite suggestive. Follow along and you will find yourself on the **Great Staircase** leading up to the Dining Hall. On the top of the stairs, before entering the Dining Hall, notice the Buttery. This is a student bar, but it was originally used as a pantry and storage place for kitchen supplies.

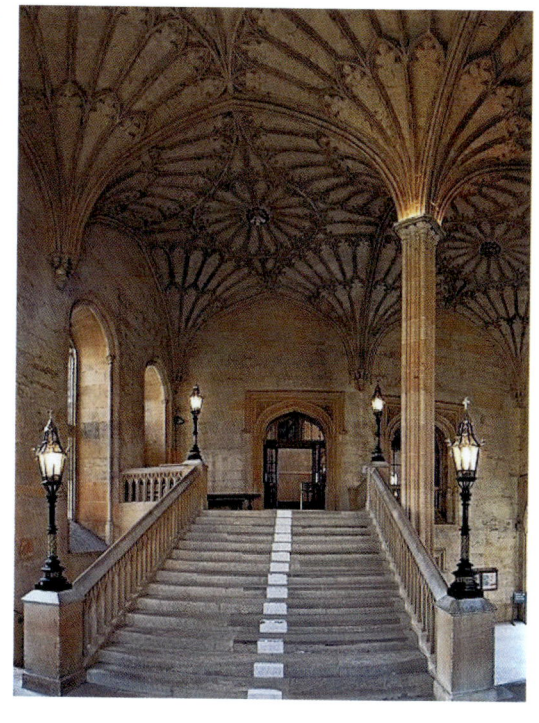

HP2.

B6. Upon entering the **Dining Hall**, please note it is a functional dining facility and in daily use. It will be closed to visitors at students' mealtimes. As you enter the Hall, you will be presented with many portraits of past and present personalities of significant importance for the college. Walk along the corridor, and halfway across on your left, look up at the stained glass window. This is dedicated to Alice in Wonderland and you will note several references to the book's characters.

Continue along to the end and reach the High Table, where professors sit for their meals. Here, you can see the portrait of Henry VIII. There is a strict connection between the King and the college. The construction of the college was the idea of Henry VIII's right-hand man, Cardinal Wolsey. The college stands on the ground of St. Frideswide's Priory. That was demolished around 1520, and work began on *Cardinal College*. But when Wolsey returned from visiting the Pope on behalf of

Henry VIII with a refusal for the divorce from his wife, the

cardinal fell out of favour, and Henry assumed responsibility for finishing the college. At this point, the college was renamed *King's College*. It then became the *House of Christ College* and eventually *Christ Church*. So, Henry VIII was directly involved with this college. So much so that he established the Diocese of Oxford and assigned the college's chapel as the **Cathedral of Oxford**.

The Dining Hall at Christ Church is famous for having been the seat of Charles I's Parliament during the English Civil War, between 1642 and 1646.
HP1.

B7. As you come out of the dining hall, you are shepherded out to the quad, past the **No Peel** graffiti on the door. There are many theories behind this inscription. One of them is that the students were made to peel potatoes and were fed up with it and complained. Another is that it was written as a protest against Robert Peel, who studied at the college and then became Prime Minister. Another one still is that students were given potato peel soup to fight fever, and they protested at the lengthy, useless cure. I suggest you select the theory that best resonates with you.

B8. As you come out in the open, you'll find yourself in **Tom Quad**, the biggest college quad in Oxford. Lewis Carroll had his room looking out on this quad. From here you have a magnificent view of Tom Tower (see point **15** of the Main Tour). Follow the indications to the **Cathedral**. On your way in, on both sides, are the names of the students and professors who perished during the two World Wars.

The dual role as cathedral and college chapel is unique in the Church of England. Oxford Cathedral is both one of the smallest cathedrals and the biggest college chapel.

The cathedral is Norman with Victorian additions, but its origins go back to the Saxon times when a church was built here around the shrine of St. Frideswide (see Castle Tour point **A4**). Her shrine was held in the Abbey of her Priory until the Abbey was destroyed during the St. Brice's Day Massacre in 1002 when the King ordered the slaughter of all the Danes. The Danish population sought refuge in the church, but this was set alight.

After this, a monastery was built on the same grounds. It is believed that the Cathedral stands on top of the Saxon Priory church.

In 1180, Frideswide's remains were moved into a new shrine in the monastery church, an event personally witnessed by Henry II. Frideswide was declared the patron saint of the city. Throughout the medieval period, the shrine of St. Frideswide was a popular place of pilgrimage, but it was heavily damaged during the Dissolution of the Monasteries under Henry VIII.

The shrine was restored under Mary I in 1588, but it was later damaged again and the saint's bones were mixed with those of a woman named Catherine Dammartin. The bones remain mixed to this day.

When Tom Quad was being built between 1525 and 1529, the original Norman church nave was pulled down. The cathedral we have today is therefore only a fraction of its original size. In 1546, the monastery church became the cathedral of the Oxford diocese at the same time as it was being absorbed into Henry's new Christ Church College.

When you enter the cathedral, you are in the chancel area. This dates back to the mid-1100s.

Toward the south, you will find the stained-glass window that depicts the martyrdom of Thomas Beckett. This dates back to the 1300s and is a rare example of medieval art, as it managed to escape Henry VIII's destruction by having the saint's face replaced by clear glass.

The centrepiece of the cathedral is Frideswide's shrine, in the Latin Chapel. The shrine dates mainly to 1289.

As you walk down, check out the grave of John de Nowers, a Norman knight who died in 1386. As you can see he was nearly 6 feet tall, a real giant for his times. His nose is white as it is considered good luck to rub it. You can try your luck too. Let me know if it works. ☺

Spend some time admiring this beautiful building and its mixed architecture.

HP4.

B9. When you come out of the Cathedral, you will have to follow the sign. The college will direct you in one of two different ways out.

1. From the Cathedral, you might be directed through the cloister, back to Tom Quad. Walk along the wall passing the entrance to the Cathedral, then proceed along the same wall. You will pass by the Dean's lodge. Look at the door and notice the knocker on the lower section. This was

allegedly added for little Alice Liddell so that she could knock at the door of her home. Continue along the wall and you will find yourself in the next quad, Peckwater Quad. This is where you will pass the College library on your right. You can then exit the college from the gate in front of you. You are now in Oriel Square. Merton Street is right ahead of you. Now you can follow the tour from step **B10** below.

2. From the Cathedral, you might be directed straight back to the main entrance of the College, where you came in. You will now be back out on Christ Church Meadow. Take a left along the College building and then left again, always keeping Christ Church

buildings on your left; you will have Magdalen School Sports Grounds on your right.

In front of you is the Merton Grove Kissing Gate. Just before you go through it, take a look to your right. This tranquil walkway with the Merton College wall (the southern wall of the Saxon fortified city) on the left and the sports ground on the right is called **Dead Man's Walk**

Until the 1300s, the area between Carfax and Christ Church, on the side of the road where the Town Hall now stands, was the Jewish settlement (see point **16**). The Jewish cemetery was where the Botanical

Garden now is. Dead Man's Walk was the route the bodies used to take on their last journey.

B10. Go through the **Kissing Gate**, and you come out on **Merton Street**, take a minute to look to your right and you will notice the old cobblestones and how the road looks to have been frozen in time.

Turn left and follow the road around the bend, then take the right fork in the road, onto tiny Oriel Street. At the end cross he High Street and rejoin the main tour at point **22,** University Church. Alternatively, take the additional itinerary to the Botanical Gardens and/or Punting Tour (Tour **C**).

Tour C: Botanical Garden and Punting

Add an extra 40 minutes to the main tour if visiting the Botanical Garden only. Punting tours start from 30 minutes.

There is a charge for visiting the Botanical Garden and punting is charged according to the length of time you hire the punt.

*From point **21** of the main tour*, outside the University Church, with the church on your left and Oriel Street to your right, continue along the High Street.

C1. Notice tiny **Magpie Lane** on your right, just before the

Old Bank Hotel. As Oxford was a very busy and bustling Saxon town, nothing was missing, it even had its red-light district. This tiny passage changed its name to the current one in the 17th century, after a pub named Magpie opened here. However, it used to be called *Gropers Lane*, clearly an indication of the activities taking place here. The original name was even worse than that!

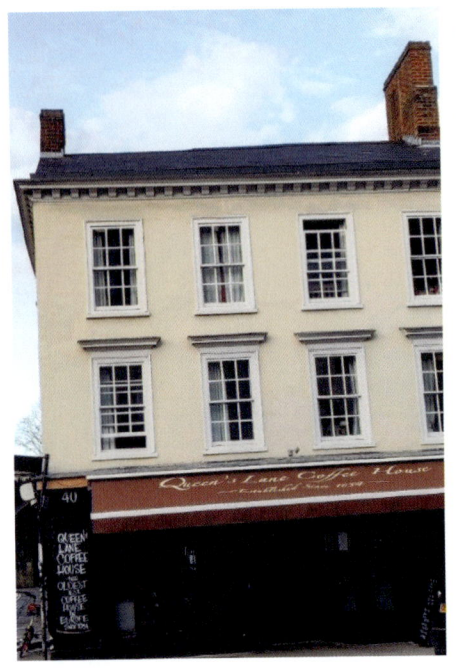

C2. Continue along the High Street and just past Queen's College on your left, on the corner of the High Street and Queen's Lane, you will find **Queen's Lane Coffee House**. Established in 1654, this is the oldest standing coffee house in Europe that has been in continuous use. It's a good place to stop for a rest and a bite to eat.

C3. Just past the *Coffee House*, on the opposite side of High Street, you will find the **Examination Schools**. Completed in 1882, this is one of the largest buildings belonging to the University. It is used for the organisation and administration of the university examinations. Many students sit their exams in this building.

The building was requisitioned during the First World War and functioned as the headquarters of the Royal Army Medical Corps, the hospital used to treat military casualties.

C4. Proceeding along High Street, look up and you will be able to see **Magdalen Tower**. This beautiful, square tower belongs to **Magdalen College**. On May Morning, the college choir sings from the top of the tower at 6 a.m., to welcome summer. May Day is a big party tradition. Big crowds gather around the tower, on the High Street and on the bridge to hear the choir, to start a celebratory day or finish a celebratory night.

Magdalen College is beautiful and dates back to the mid-1400s. Its famous alumni include Oscar Wilde and C.S. Lewis. The grounds are magnificent and home to the only "vegetable deer" in the world. There is a small charge to visit the college, but if time permits, it is well worth it. The extensive park runs along the river Cherwell and lends itself to a superb walk. In the field, you will spot the college's fallow deer. In the years after World War II, when the country was on its knees, meat was rationed. The college managed to classify its deer as *vegetables*, so that they would not be confiscated. Now, that's what I call creative!

Once out of the college main Porter's Lodge, cross High Street.

C5. You are now in front of the **Botanical Garden**. This is the first Botanical Garden in the UK and was founded in 1621. It stands on the site of the old Jewish cemetery (see points **16** and **B9**).

The garden houses nearly 6,000 different types of plant and its biodiversity is a feast for the eyes all year around.

There is a charge to enter the garden, but it is well worth a visit. With glasshouses, walled gardens, borders and gardens, this place is a dream.

The Botanical Garden is also featured in many literary works. Not only it was a place often visited by Charles Dodgson (a.k.a. Lewis Carroll) and the Liddell family and served as inspiration for many Alice in Wonderland adventures, it is also the place where J.R.R. Tolkien used to come to gather thoughts for his famous books. The Botanical Garden is also mentioned in the first chapter of Evelyn Waugh's *Brideshead Revisited*, where Lord Sebastian brings Charles Ryder "to see the ivy". In Philip Pullman's trilogy *His Dark Materials*, a bench in the garden is the place that the two parallel worlds have in common and where its protagonists, Lyra and Will, can hope to feel each other's presence. The bench has now become a place of pilgrimage for Pullman's fans, and it is recognisable by the "*Lyra + Will*" graffiti left by them.

C6. When you exit the gardens, cross back over High Street and turn right toward the bridge. Just before you reach it, dip left and go on a punting adventure.

Punting is a very typical Oxfordian activity. It consists of a long, wooden boat, being propelled forward (hopefully) by pushing a long pole into the riverbed. If this sounds too much like hard work, you can hire a punt with a chauffeur, and sit back and enjoy the beautiful sights as you slowly cruise along.

As there is a charge for punting and it is only really enjoyable if the weather is magnanimous, it is very much up to you if you want to indulge in this activity. If you do not feel like trying it, just take a picture of the punts and pretend you have been on one.

Now retrace your steps along the High Street, back to the University Church, and rejoin the main tour at point **22**.

Tour D: New College

Add an extra 30 minutes to the main tour.

The college charges an entry fee (£5 per person at the time of writing).

From point **32** of the main tour.

Exit the Bodleian library area and pass under the Bridge of Sighs. Continue along New College Lane until you get to the entrance of the college.

The name of the college is indeed misleading as New College is one of the oldest ones in town. The reason for its name is that when it was built, it was called St. Mary College. At the time, there was already an existing St. Mary College – subsequently renamed Oriel College, and therefore this one was the *New* one. The college was built after the Black Death, which peaked between 1347 and 1351 and caused the death of a high percentage of the population (between 75 and 200 million individuals across Europe and Asia, depending on the source). Many of the people who died were religious figures and there was, therefore, a very urgent need to rebuild this stratum of the population. Educating the new generation of priests became a priority. William of Wykeham, the Bishop of Winchester, set about addressing this issue by buying cheap grounds – mainly belonging to what are now Merton and Queen's Colleges on the north-east edge of the walled city. This land was primarily the City Ditch and had been used as a burial ground during the Black Death. It was described by a jury in 1379 as "full of filth, dirt and stinking carcasses...[a] concourse of malefactors, murderers, whores and thieves". William cleared the area and founded the college in 1379.

The motto of the College is "*Manners Makyth Man*", which was revolutionary, not only because it was in English rather than Latin, but especially because it made a social statement; it is not by birth, money or property that an individual is defined, but by how he or she behaves toward other people. This is reminiscent of Aristotle's motto that what we do is what we are.

D1. As you enter the college from New College Lane, the entrance to the Chapel and Cloister will be to your immediate left, but if you follow the Chapel wall along the quad to the ascending staircase in the next corner, you will find yourself in the **Dining Hall**. This is fully functional and will be closed during students' meal times.

William Wykeham's charter stated that wrestling, dancing and "all noisy games" were forbidden in the hall because of its close proximity to the college chapel. The charter also prescribed the use of Latin in conversation.

The original flooring was replaced by the present marble flooring in 1722 and in 1865 the open oak roof was restored, after being replaced by a ceiling for nearly a century.

HP1.

D2. On exiting the Hall, descend the stone stairs and turn left, then left again under the arch, and walk to the iron gate to the garden. The **Garden** of the College now incorporates the city walls; originally it was enclosed by it. You can still see the Saxon wall as you step into the garden. As the college was allowed to use the city wall, it also had to maintain it. The King or Queen inspected the walls every three years to ensure that it was kept robust and in good state of repair. Nowadays, the Major of Oxford does exactly the same things, carrying out a centuries-old tradition.

The students of New College also sign up to agree that they can be called to defend the wall in case of an attempted invasion. Students, be warned!

HP7.

D3. Retrace your steps back to the first quad and make your way the **Chapel.** This is stunning. Its choir ranks amongst the top world choirs and has recorded more than one hundred albums.

Take the time to visit this T-shaped structure and admire the stained glass windows and the statues that adorn it.

D4. On exiting the Chapel, turn right and you'll find yourself in the **Cloister.** This is a beautiful structure built to ensure that religious studies were facilitated by meditation and dates back to the 1400s. In its centre, there is a 200 year old European oak tree. The cloister and its corridors have featured heavily in several films. For Harry Potter fans, this is where the "ferret scene" was filmed in the *Goblet of Fire*.

HP5, HP6.

Upon exiting the college, retrace your steps down New College Lane, and at the Bridge of Sighs, rejoin the Main Tour at point **33**.

Tour E: Natural History and Pitt Rivers Museums

Add an extra 60 minutes to the main tour if you are visiting both museums. Please bear in mind that it might take you a lot longer for an in-depth visit as the collections are very extensive.

There is no cost associated with this secondary tour. All museums in Oxford are free.

*From point **36** of the Main Tour*, turn right onto Parks Road, leaving the Kings Arms pub on your right and the Weston Library on your left. Continue on Parks Road and cross at the traffic light. On your right-hand side, you will soon see the Natural History Museum building.

E1. The **University Museum of Natural History** is a fantastic-looking building dating back to between 1855 and 1860 when Sir Henry Acland, Professor of Medicine, initiated construction of the museum to bring together all the aspects of science around a central display area. Until then, the facilities for teaching natural science were scattered around the city in various colleges, as were the anatomical and natural history specimens.

The building was financed through the sale of Bibles. Several departments moved into it, but, as the departments grew in size, they had to move out to purpose-built facilities along South Park Road.

The museum consists of a large square court with a glass roof supported by cast-iron pillars. Around the ground floor and the first floor there are cloister-like corridors with stone columns, each made from a different British stone.

The Natural History museum has the most complete specimen of the dodo, a flightless bird that went extinct in the 17th century. The museum has one of the bird's mummified skulls, and bones from the foot and leg.

E2. Inside the Natural History Museum, through a door on the opposite side to the main entrance, you will find the **Pitt Rivers Museum.** This building was added between 1885 and 1886 to house the collections of Augustus Pitt Rivers, who donated them to the university with the understanding that *anthropology* would be offered as a subject. The Pitt Rivers Museum is a treasure trove of all sorts of things collected by Pitt Rivers in his extensive journeys over several years. You can spend hours in this overcrowded, dimly lit Pandora's Box! If you are visiting with children, ask for a torch and a treasure trail. The little ones will spend hours finding the toy mice hidden in the museum.

E3. Exit the main museum building and take a look at the dinosaur footprints on the lawn. These are replicas of the ones found in limestone in Ardley, 20 Km from Oxford.

Now, look across the road at **Keble College**. With its distinctive neogothic red brick design, this 1870 college is famous for breaking the tradition of arranging rooms along staircases and using corridors instead. **HP1.**

E4. If you have time before sundown, take a walk in the fantastic **University Parks**. With the museum behind you, turn right and you will find the fence to the park and one of the main gates. Have a stroll down to the river and admire the beautiful flower borders and fields. If this extra walk is not for you, then turn left outside the museum and retrace your steps back to point **37** of the Main Tour.

Tour F: Exeter College

Add an extra 20 minutes to the main tour.

There is no charge for this tour.

F1. *From point 42 of the end of the Main Tour,* cross Broad Street toward the statue on the roof and take **Turl Street**. This strange name comes from there being a *twirling* gate here as an entrance to the old city. The gate was demolished in 1722.

Just past Ship Street on the right, you'll see the entrance gate to Exeter College to your left.

F2. **Exeter College** is usually open to the public in the afternoon (after 2pm) and is free to visit. It is well-worth visiting as it is a stunning college. On entering the main quad, you will find the **chapel** to your left. Spend some time visiting it; it is incredibly beautiful.

F3. As you come out of the chapel, head left and then right around the quad. Nearly diagonal from the chapel is the entrance to the **Fellows' Garden**. Venture in and cross it until you encounter some ascending stairs. You will find yourself on a terrace overlooking Radcliffe Square (point **23**), with incredible views of the Camera, the University Church and the Bodleian Library.

On your way out of Exeter College, turn right at the Porter's Lodge and find yourself back on Broad Street. Turn left here and before arriving at the Tourist Information Centre; you will pass an **Oxfam Shop.** Cross the road and rejoin the main tour at point **43**.

The Harry Potter Connection

What is the connection between Harry Potter and Oxford?

Oxford served as a great inspiration for a lot of the Harry Potter books and films, as well as the setting of some great scenes.

J.K. Rowling did not study at Oxford University (not for want of trying), but she did live in Oxford for two years after graduating. She was therefore very well acquainted with the many nooks and crannies that make up this ancient city.

The following list points out the strict connections between Oxford and Harry Potter. If you only want to visit the sites related to Harry Potter, I suggest you take the Christ Church (Tour B) and New College (Tours D) itineraries. However, the sites related to Harry Potter have been marked with **HP** throughout the different tours, so you can find information about them here.

HP1. While the **Great Hall** was not filmed in any of the colleges, the real dining hall of three of them served as inspiration for the one built in the film studios: New College (see **D1**), Christ Church College (see **B6**) and Keble College (see **E3**).

HP2. Christ Church **Staircase** (see **B5**) leading up to the Dining Hall was used in several films, it is most famous for the scene of the arrival of the students to Hogwarts, in the Philosopher's Stone, when Professor McGonagall stands tapping her fingers at the top of the stairs as the new students arrive.

HP3. Christ Church **Cloisters** were also used in Harry Potter. The space just outside the gift shop is where Hermione tells Harry that he has Quidditch in his blood and shows him his father's medal in the cabinet.

HP4. The **baptismal font** that can be found in Christ Church Cathedral (see **B8**), is the inspiration behind the Pensee in Professor Dumbledore's office.

HP5. New College Cloister (see **D5**) was the setting for the scene where Draco Malfoy gets turned into a ferret by Mad Eye Moody, in *The Goblet of Fire*. Fans will recognise the majestic tree in the middle as the one Malfoy was sitting on at the beginning of the scene.

HP6. New College Cloisters have also been used extensively in the Harry Potter series for the **corridor scenes**.

HP7. The **old city wall in New College Garden** (see **D2**) was used as a background for many scenes.

HP8. The **Divinity School** (point **29**), at the Bodleian Library was used as the Infirmary Wing at Hogwarts. It was also used in the scene where Ron has to learn to dance with Professor McGonagall.

~ Oxford in One Afternoon ~

HP9. The locking mechanism of **Thomas Bodley Chest** (point **29**) was the inspiration for the Vault.

HP10. The **Duke of Humphrey Library**, just above the Divinity School, is where the *restricted* area of the library was filmed in Harry Potter. You can visit this library only with a Bodleian Library own tour.

HP11. The statue of the **Duke of Pembroke** (see point **28**), in the Central Quad of the Bodleian Library, was the inspiration for Nearly Headless Nick.

HP12. The **Turf Tavern** (point **33**) served not only as the inspiration for the Leaking Cauldron, but was also often frequented by the crew during the filming.

HP13. When visiting **University Church** (point **22**), check out the ceiling in the main sector, near the organ. The blue sky with golden stars inspired the dining hall ceiling at Hogwarts in Harry Potter.

HP14. A mason's signature on the stone flooring outside the **Sheldonian Theatre** (see point **31**), near the exit toward Broad Street, was the inspiration for Harry's scar. You can see at least three of them in the yard just between the Theatre building and the Heads.

HP 15. You can watch a match of **Quidditch** in Oxford University Parks, where the teams train on Wednesdays and Saturdays. Although these teams do not fly around the pitch, they do run around with a stick between their legs, chasing a snitch.

HP16. And of course, you know that **Emma Watson** was born and raised in Oxford, right? She also famously said that IF (not when, but IF) she were to ever get married, she would do so in the Divinity School.

~ Oxford in One Afternoon ~

40 Facts about Oxford

Apart from the Colleges and University, what is Oxford famous for? What other things are worth knowing? Well, quite a lot, actually. Take a peep at the list below.

1. The Mini Car. A big part of eastern Oxford was built around the Morris Motors factory in Cowley.

2. Wild horses roam Port Meadow, a large expanse of ground along the river in the North area of Oxford.

3. There is a yearly carnival held in Oxford. Cowley Road Carnival usually falls on the first Sunday in July and is a happy and noisy occasion.

4. Currently approximately 40% of Oxford University students are not from the UK.

5. The symbol of the city is a bull (or ox) on water. This is because the original name of Oxford is, in fact, *Oxanforda,* or *Oxenforde,* the place where cattle could cross the river and be taken to London to be traded. The exact location of the *ford* is disputed, but it is likely to be somewhere near Folly Bridge, at the bottom of St. Aldates.

6. There is a yearly street fair which originated in 1200 when St. Giles Church was consecrated. St. Giles Fair is a two-day event held on the Monday and Tuesday after the Sunday following 1 September. It's a major event that sees one of the main arteries of the city closed for two days.

7. Oxford was the capital of England for four years, between 1642 and 1646, during the Civil War, when Charles I hid in Christ Church and held his Parliament in the Great Hall, while Oliver Cromwell besieged the city (see point **B6**).

8. Oxford has the only deer classified as vegetables (see point **C4**)

9. Hitler intended Oxford to be his capital once his plan of conquering the Europe was accomplished. Thanks to that, Oxford was never bombed during the War, as opposed to London, which was blitzed. This means that Oxford has not suffered any damage to its historical buildings.

10. At least 28 Prime Ministers throughout the centuries studied at Oxford (too many to name).

11. Oxford and Cambridge were the only educational institutions in England until the mid-1800s, when Durham University and University College London were established.

12. Oxford gets more than 10 million visitors a year.

13. The resident population is just over 150,000 and the number of students at the University of Oxford (in colleges and private halls) is around 24,000; approximately 50% undergraduates and 50% graduates.

14. Women were first allowed to study at Oxford University in 1878 but could not obtain a degree till 1920, and it wasn't until 1974 that the last of the all-male colleges opened its doors to female students.

15. Oxford University is made up of 39 colleges (the newest one is Parks College, opened in 2019) and 6 private halls.

16. Oxford is not a private university. It is open to anyone who can comply with its high requirements.

17. There is another very large university in the city: Oxford Brookes University, with a student population of more than 18,000.

18. 28 Nobel Prize Winners studied at Oxford University.

19. Oxford has been the setting for many films – here is just a small selection: X-Men: First Class, Howard's End, Harry Potter, Brideshead Revisited, Saving Private Ryan, A Fish Called Wanda, 102 Dalmatians and The Italian Job.

20. Colin Dexter's character, *Inspector Morse*, was based in Oxford. The books inspired a long television series and two additional spin off series: *Lewis* and *Endeavour*. All are set in the heart of Oxford.

21. Roger Bannister, a 25-year-old medical student, was the first person to run the mile in less than four minutes. He set the record in 1954 at the Iffley Sports Ground in Oxford with a time of 3 minutes, 59.4 seconds.

22. Many countries have adopted an "Oxford". There is an Oxford in New Zealand, one in Canada, 21 in the United States, two Lake Oxfords, and a Mount Oxford.

23. There is an Oxford blue – being a dark blue colour.

24. There is also an Oxford marmalade, made by Frank Cooper's company for more than 100 years.

25. The word "snob" originated in Oxford, and it comes from the Latin phrase "sine nobilitate" which means "without nobility."

26. The Holywell Music Room (1748) is the oldest music performance hall in Europe.

27. Oxford has more published authors per square mile than anywhere else in the world.

28. The Queen's Lane Coffee House is the oldest continually operating coffee house in Europe (see point **C2**).

29. There are about six applicants for each available space at Oxford.

30. A 25-foot headless *shark* is sticking out of a roof in a house in the Headington area of Oxford. This was erected in 1986 by the American presenter Bill Heine, owner of the house, as a protest against the Cold War.

31. Two of the biggest colleges, Trinity and Balliol, hold tortoise races every year. Each college has a tortoise that is looked after by dedicated students. Every year, they are placed in the centre of a circle made of lettuce leaves. The tortoise that reaches the lettuce first wins.

32. In Oxford there are two roads off the main artery that runs from the centre to the North of the city. One is called North Parade and the other South Parade. Confusingly, North Parade is farther south than South Parade. This is because during the Civil War, while Cromwell was besieging Charles I, North Parade was the farthest north territory governed by Charles I, while South Parade, was the southernmost area occupied by Cromwell. The area that is now between the two roads was an open battle ground.

33. Academics studying at the Bodleian Library didn't have heating until 1845 and lighting until 1929.

34. When you study at Oxford University you must belong to a college. You would usually apply to a specific college, but might be given a place in another. It is all a question of numbers. All colleges require the same level of entrance. You can indeed also send an open application and accept whichever college placement you are given.

35. As most colleges offer most subjects, because you study at the university faculty and not the college itself, the choice of the college is not only down to academic reputation. The choice is influenced by factors like the political orientation of the college, its choir (if you are musically inclined), its sports teams (if you are into that), its physical location (you might prefer one side of town to another), its size (some colleges are smaller and cosier), its fame with tourists (you might not enjoy being surrounded by visitors while pursuing your studies), etc

36. The faces and figures adorning most of the college buildings have inspired many literary characters and are both funny and disturbing. But what are they called? If they have a function, i.e. they spout water out of the gutters then they are called Gargoyles. If they are just adorning the walls and have no specific function (as with most of them), they are called Grotesques.

37. Which rivers run through Oxford? Well, the Cherwell and the Isis, of course. *Not the Thames?* I hear you wondering. This is one of the many areas where Oxford's eccentricity comes through. The original name for the river was *Tamesis*, i.e. wide waters, in Latin. While in Oxford it is known as the Isis, the other 215 miles know it as the River Thames. One and the same, indeed.

38. Stephen Hawking was born in Oxford in 1942 and graduated from University College, Oxford, before moving to Cambridge for his PhD.

39. There is an Oxford Comma, don't you know? For the pedantic English language perfectionists, the *Oxford Comma* is put before a conjunction (for example *and, or*) in lists of three or more. For example, "the good, the bad and the ugly", would be "the good, the bad, and the ugly."

40. The number one crime in Oxford is bicycle theft.

List of Colleges in 2019

U=Undergraduates • P=Postgraduates/Fellows • V=Visiting students • M=Male students • F=Female students • T=Total students – Number of students in 2015

Name	Year	Total assets £'000 2017-18	U	P	V	M%	F%	T
All Souls College	1438	461,343	0	6	0	67	33	6
Balliol College	1263	139,314	373	279	3	60	40	655
Brasenose College	1509	176,283	367	203	3	56	44	573
Christ Church	1546	564,173	428	164	1	59	41	593
Corpus Christi College	1517	178,827	249	94	0	55	45	343
Exeter College	1314	128,791	316	186	25	55	45	527
Green Templeton College	2008	99,218	101	441	0	47	53	542
Harris Manchester College	1786 College: 1996	41,038	82	134	1	48	52	217
Hertford College	1282 College: 1740	84,409	394	204	24	48	52	622
Jesus College	1571	211,687	330	185	2	56	44	517
Keble College	1870	127,403	416	227	4	61	39	647
Kellogg College	1990 College: 1994	N/A	0	905	0	62	38	905
Lady Margaret Hall	1878	66,480	395	213	13	50	50	621
Linacre College	1962	30,418	0	437	0	53	47	437

Name	Year	Total assets £'000 2017-18	U	P	V	M%	F%	T
Lincoln College	1427	156,548	297	316	4	51	49	617
Magdalen College	1458	309,052	393	176	4	59	41	573
Mansfield College	1886 College: 1995	31,347	220	130	35	56	44	385
Merton College	1264	286,846	291	253	1	56	44	545
New College	1379	307,806	429	256	13	55	45	698
Nuffield College	1937	256,054	0	81	0	58	42	81
Oriel College	1326	96,728	325	172	4	55	45	501
Parks College	2019	N/A	0	0	0	0	0	0
Pembroke College	1624	86,131	365	227	35	56	44	627
The Queen's College	1341	368,051	342	138	4	53	47	484
St Anne's College	1879 College: 1952	68,565	423	322	33	50	50	778
St Antony's College	1950 College: 1963	72,551	0	451	2	49	51	453
St Catherine's College	1963	114,531	476	387	45	55	45	908
St Cross College	1965	N/A	0	557	1	53	47	558
St Edmund Hall	1278 College: 1957	80,913	404	291	24	56	44	719
St Hilda's College	1893	113,407	411	163	2	51	49	576
St Hugh's College	1886	70,728	432	333	3	55	45	768
St John's College	1555	631,615	385	221	1	55	45	607

Name	Year	Total assets £'000 2017-18	U	P	V	M%	F%	T
St Peter's College	1929	64,319	340	188	24	54	46	552
Somerville college	1879	224,951	385	171	0	49	51	556
Trinity College	1555	163,787	286	136	2	55	45	424
University College	1249	206,920	363	199	1	58	42	563
Wadham College	1610	137,983	451	166	33	54	46	650
Wolfson College	1966 College: 1981	78,141	0	555	0	57	43	555
Worcester College	1714	83,179	428	146	27	49	51	**601**
Total		6,319,537	10,897	9,713	374	54	46	20,984

Source: Wikipedia - Colleges of the University of Oxford

Please note, this table does not include the six Private Halls.

Author's Note

I hope you enjoyed discovering this magnificent city as much as I love living here. I have carried out extensive research into the background and history of the various places mentioned in the itineraries to ensure I give you the most in-depth and accurate information on them. As we go back over a few centuries of history and legends, please forgive any slight inaccuracy that might have made its way into this guide.

The timings for the tours are to be taken as guidelines only. Please note that it might take you longer to visit all the places along the itineraries.

If you wish to contact me to discuss the guide, to book a tour of the city with me or for any other reason, please email me at renlan.uk@gmail.com and put *OXFORD* as the subject. You can also contact me via the **Renata Lanzoni** Facebook page.

Thank you for taking the time to get to know Oxford.

Other Books by the Author

<u>Non-fiction</u>:

The Light-Packer Guide

<u>Fiction</u>:

Shattered Moon

Printed in Poland
by Amazon Fulfillment
Poland Sp. z o.o., Wrocław